Dulha Rai's Conquest of Dausa

Dulha Rai's Conquest of Dausa

THE EARLY HISTORY OF KACHWAHAS

Maharaj Devraj Singh

RUPA

Published by
Rupa Publications India Pvt. Ltd 2022
7/16, Ansari Road, Daryaganj
New Delhi 110002

Sales centres:
Allahabad Bengaluru Chennai
Hyderabad Jaipur Kathmandu
Kolkata Mumbai

P-ISBN: 978-93-5520-629-9
E-ISBN: 978-93-5520-870-5

First impression 2022

10 9 8 7 6 5 4 3 2 1

Printed in India

CONTENTS

FOREWORD

राजनाथ सिंह
RAJNATH SINGH

सत्यमेव जयते

गृह मंत्री
भारत
नई दिल्ली-110001
HOME MINISTER
INDIA
NEW DELHI-110001

Message

I am glad to know that **The Maharaj Shri Devraj Singh of Jaipur (Rajasthan)** has written a book on the early history of the Kachwaha Rajputs, who during the early-medieval period were known as the Kachaphaghatas of Gwalior and Narwar. I believe this book titled **"Dulha Rai's Conquest of Dausa: The Early History of the Kachwahas"** would be an important addition to the history of The Kachwahas.

I congratulate Maharaj Shri Devraj Singh for the publication of the book and wish it's successful reception.

With good wishes,

(Rajnath Singh)

Office : Room No. 104, Ministry of Home Affairs, North Block, New Delhi-110 001
Tel. : 23092462, 23094686, Fax : 23094221
E-mail : hm@nic.in

INTRODUCTION

Meeting with a group of students at a function outside Jaipur a few years ago, it occurred to me that the majority of them were hardly aware of the history of the erstwhile Jaipur State, also known as the kingdom of Dhundhar (also spelt Dhoondhar). They had certainly heard of some of the more famous maharajas, great ranas, nawabs and rawals of lore who had ruled in bygone eras. Nonetheless, the chronicle of the state that gave shelter to their families for generations, and whose capital now also serves as the state capital of Rajasthan, was something akin to ancient history as far as these young students were concerned. The fact, though, is that it is far from ancient. It has, however, been 73 years now since my grandfather Maharaja Sawai Man Singh II of the erstwhile princely state of Jaipur agreed to merge with the Indian Union in the fateful year of 1949. Perhaps today's youth is not aware of the fact that the Indian rulers who sacrificed their hereditary ruling rights for what they believed to be the progress and prosperity of the Indian Union were, in

1949, rightly hailed and acknowledged as the 'co-architects of modern India'. As Dhananajaya Singh writes in his book *The House of Marwar: The Story of Jodhpur*, the accession of the Indian princely states into the Indian Union were 'the very first set of contracts signed and sealed by this fledging nation, and that too with a group of people who together contributed in more territory than Jinnah had taken away...'[1]

What troubled me further was the fact that the name Dhundhar, as the Kachwaha kingdom in Rajasthan was known, is fading from the memory of the younger generation. For people from outside of Rajasthan, the name of Dhundhar would certainly be unfamiliar, as even Rajwarra, the old name by which Rajasthan was known, also seems to be disappearing from public memory. (In terms of usage, 'Rajputana' fares slightly better.) This was perplexing to me, as, after all, prior to the merger of the princely states into the Indian Union, it was an acknowledged fact that the Rajput states (not only those of Rajputana) were the most enduring political institutions in South Asia, and certainly in north India.

That the term 'Dhundhar' is lesser heard today may partly be due to the fact that the Dhund River, like the Saraswati of yore, has now disappeared completely due to geological changes. The Dhundhari dialect, which my forefathers as well as my own father uttered with pride, is also dying and being heard less and less. Additionally, it was the custom of the British, during the nineteenth century, to simplify the names of various Indian kingdoms by referring to them by the name

[1]Singh, Dhananajaya, *The House of Marwar: The Story of Jodhpur*, Roli Books, New Delhi, 1994, p. 12.

of their capital city, thus rendering the old names increasingly less prominent in terms of practical usage.

One consolation is that the names of important (or colourful) rulers are still recognized by the people of the erstwhile states and are often fondly recounted at dinner parties. Oral history, storytelling within the family/community and bardic ballads are ways in which the majority of the populace have retained knowledge of their rich heritage.

Indeed, it was a tradition not only in Rajasthan but much of India that oral history passed down generations served as a means of recording important events, propagating a ruler's achievements (and the legitimacy of the ruling clans), among other traditional knowledge. Musician groups such as the Langas and the Manganiyars were often employed by patrons (jajmans) for remembering the past and for maintenance of genealogies. It is quite common to find these genealogists able to recite back 14 to 18 generations of their patron family's past. Then there is another kind of genealogists, the Bhats, who are divided into the Mukhbancha Bhat and the Pothibancha Bhat. While the former relies entirely on the memorization of oral tradition, the latter maintains a written record as well.[2]

With the advent of the internet, the information age and artificial intelligence, such traditional means of storytelling and genealogical record-keeping are facing an uncertain future.

---

[2]Bharucha, Rustom, *Rajasthan: An Oral History: Conversations with Komal Kothari*, Penguin Books, 2003, pp. 28–29.

Another means by which history is keenly remembered in Rajasthan is through tourism. For the local youth, it is often a matter of pride when one informs a visitor about the names and legends associated with a historic place. (From my personal experience, the accuracy of the information relayed is quite often debatable, but that doesn't seem to dampen the enthusiasm of the local guides.) Tourism is an important industry in Rajasthan, which not only generates revenue for many sectors involved and offers employment opportunities but also helps to propagate local history to visitors from other parts of India and the outside world alike.

After some reflection on the decline in historical interest and knowledge among Rajasthani youth, I came to the conclusion that in order to generate interest in Dhundhar, a re-examination of its founding history and associated sites of interests was important. While the history of Jaipur and the 24 rulers of Amber are undoubtedly a matter of great interest, the subject has been touched upon by other books. This book aims to focus on the period which predates the capture and establishment of Amber as the capital of Dhundhar by Rao Kakildeva (Kakil). So, we turn our attention to the first capital of Dhundhar, the fort of Dausa, for it is in this historic locality that the story of the Kachwahas in Rajasthan began. The story of Dausa is, after all, significantly linked to the founding history of Dhundhar (hence Jaipur State). It begins with the legend of Dulha Rai, the 'bridegroom prince', and it is his world that I shall attempt to present to the readers here.

Situated nearly 60 kilometres south-east of Jaipur towards Uttar Pradesh/Madhya Pradesh and bordering Alwar,

Bharatpur, Karuali and Sawai Madhopur, I first got to visit the district of Dausa, its historic fort as well as other local places of interests in the year 2011. I was warmly welcomed by the residents, and it was truly a memorable visit for me.

Although the district of Dausa gained its name from this ancient fortification, the fort of Dausa remains a site rarely visited by outsiders, despite its historical importance and interesting background. The reason why this ancient fort has remained outside the tourists' radar became obvious to me upon inspection. The local population, particularly the younger generation that today constitutes over 50 per cent of the population in India, hardly knows about the historical importance of Dausa garh or fort, and so it is no wonder that casual local/foreign tourists have barely heard of or considered visiting it. It was this lack of awareness among the local youth of Dausa and beyond about the rich history and culture of the place that inspired me to begin work on this book. My hope is that this book will play a small part in encouraging the local youth to become more desirous of learning their own history, and if it inadvertently helps to generate tourism (hence, much-needed employment/income diversification for the locals of Dausa), then, by all means, I would consider it a success.

It must be admitted that no first-hand material survives from the period when Dausa served as the first capital of Dhundhar, apart from the walls, bricks, mortars and baoris (stepwells) themselves. It is a period closer to what historians today refer to as 'early medieval India', which, unlike the late medieval period, was not yet influenced by Persianized culture, known for recording history with exact chronology and in minute detail. Most of what is known today include the chronological names of the rulers, the approximate dates they ruled and the places they ruled from. Among the most important document that gives the clan's own annals of its history is the *Kachhawan Ri Vanshavali*. According to Shyam Singh Ratnawat, who searched extensively for copies of this manuscript in Jaipur, Jodhpur and Udaipur, the majority of *Kachhawan Ri Vanshavali* in existence seems to have been created/standardized (and possibly distributed) by Maharaja Sawai Jai Singh II, who was a great collector/bibliophile by any standards and was also famous for his love of truth, knowledge and science. These copies of the *Kachhawan Ri Vanshavali* were based on whatever family records had been preserved as well as the collective memory of the clan. Another early written record that mentions the history of the clan is the *Nainsi Ri Khyat* (also known as Nainsi's Khyat), believed to have been written in the second half of the seventeenth century. There will hence be references to both the *Kachhawan Ri Vanshavali* and *Nainsi Ri Khyat* throughout this book.

In our modern times, my own grandfather also attempted to present an accurate account of Dhundhar's history by commissioning the renowned historian Sir Jadunath Sarkar, whose efforts during 1939–40 resulted in his *A History of Jaipur*. Sir Sarkar is said to have been delighted to write the book, having received full access to the archives of the Pothikhana in the City Palace, Jaipur, which at that time still retained the complete collection handed down by my forefathers. Due to his position as a prominent Indian historian, he understandably chose to concentrate his writing in areas in which there was ample first-hand as well as second-hand material, beginning with the period of Rao Prithviraj of Amber, by which time Amber had, for over four centuries, been the capital of Dhundhar Raj.

The manner in which Dausa came into Kachwaha possession is attributed to be the deed of the bridegroom prince Dulha Rai (r. 1006–1036), who is also considered to be the progenitor or first in line of the Kachwaha rulers in Dhundhar. It soon became apparent to me that the story of his life and the conquest of Dausa were rather confusing, much being based on oral history and bardic ballads that were composed centuries after his demise. More importantly, his family background was a matter not clearly demonstrated and deeply explored upon. Therefore, although this book began as a research into the history of Dausa's fort and district, it soon also came to encompass the exploration of the clan's early history, prior to their conquest of Dausa and its vicinity, during which time, they were known as the Kachaphaghatas of Gopaksetra. I was, therefore, compelled to do research into a history of the Kachaphaghatas and was thankful to have found some relevant epigraphic records and temple inscriptions, which have been of great value in shedding light on the early history of the clan. It must be noted that the mention of the Kachaphaghatas and their domain can be found scattered in history books, academic papers as well as a small number of publications, such as *Temples of Gopaksetra: A Regional History of Architecture and Sculpture in Central India* AD *600–900* by historian Michael D. Willis (1997) or *Kachchhapaghata Art and Architecture* by Ahmed Ali (2005). However, their history specifically has yet to be written, and it is my hope that this work would be of some interest to readers but would also help to fill this gap and illuminate this lesser-known period of north India's early medieval era. By doing so, I hope this would also be reflective of the Kachwaha motto, *Yato Dharma Stato Jayah* or 'Where there is (light of) Dharma, there is victory'.

I have taken the liberty to shorten the name of the clan and its varied confusion of different spellings into Kachaphaghata for the early medieval period, and Kachwaha for the medieval/Mughal period (till the present).

Interestingly, but not unique to Indian history, I have found that apart from the epigraphic records, which are rather scant as well as concise, some of the earliest written references to the Kachaphaghatas are the records of their enemies, both Hindus and Muslims.

In telling this story about an important era in Indian history such that it allows a deeper understanding of the scenarios and environs during the founding age of Dhundhar Raj, it would be necessary to foray into the characteristics of the period described as 'early medieval' as opposed to 'medieval', which, in the north Indian context, is generally marked by the inception of the Delhi Sultanate. We, therefore, go as far back as the period following the decline of the Guptas through to the rise of the Rajput states in north India. Emphasis would be retained on the abridged history of Gopaksetra in central India, which was the region in which the Kachaphagatas ruled.

We then move to what could be described as early history

of the Kachwahas (or the Kachaphaghatas). Here, we delve into what is known about their role in north Indian politics prior to the establishment of Dausa as Dulha Rai's capital. It is admittedly a matter of putting together differing pieces of the clues scattered about here and there, and piecing them together like a puzzle, in which, only then, a broader picture of this obscure period emerges. While, in doing so, I have used many quotes from qualified historians, in order to sanctify the accuracy of the narrative, the analysis of the various sources is mine. If there are any mistakes, it could be safely pledged that it was omitted unintentionally. Moreover, this section, by no means, gives a definitive history of the clan prior to its move into Rajasthan. Indeed, much remains unwritten and could be corrected or expanded upon with further research. Apart from shedding some light onto information that was hitherto generally unknown about this clan, it will also be useful in understanding the circumstances of the era and the manner in which Dausa was established as the first capital of the Kachwahas.

Having explored the early history of the Kachwahas, we will then shift our attention to the life and story of the progenitor of the Dhundhar Raj, Dulha Rai. For this, I have relied on two major texts that were penned down centuries later: the first being the version recounted by the Kachwahas themselves based on the *Kachhawan Ri Vanshavali* and the second being the popular version of James Tod, *Annals and Antiquities of Rajasthan.* In doing so, it is my hope to clear away some of the discrepancies and conflicting accounts of his life and his achievements that led to the founding of the Dhundhar Raj.

I then offer a brief historic survey of the district and township of Dausa. My search for a recent publication specifically on the history of Dausa didn't meet positive results, and it was this void that prompted me to write this section of the book—I felt it was long overdue. In order to get an overall history of the district, one is required to study the political scenario of eastern Rajasthan as a whole, from the time Dausa formed a part of the state of Matsyadesha through to the time of Dhundhar Raj.

It must be added, however, that I have just given brief descriptions of historical sites of interest that I visited during my survey. The history of the fort and district of Dausa shall be complemented with some original photos that were taken on my Leica camera.

Lastly, I would like to state that history—especially Indian history—has always been of great fascination to me. This book is the labour of love of a history enthusiast, and I hope the readers would forgive me for any mistakes/errors that may be present in this book. I am grateful to my grandparents for instilling a love of history and culture in me. I would like to thank my parents and sister, Lalitya Kumari Jaipur, for supporting me in the writing of this book. This work would not have been possible without the help of Rom P, who assisted me with research and editing, Prow P, who advised me on the meaning of Sanskrit terminologies, and Rudra Sharma and Upama Biswas at Rupa Publications.

Maharaj Devraj Singh of Jaipur
Jaipur, July 2022

ONE

EARLY MEDIEVAL NORTH INDIA

Before we chart the microcosm of the Kachwaha kingdom's early history, it is necessary to examine the macrocosm of north Indian political and dynastic history that gave rise to the circumstances, culture and environs of Dulha Rai's time. Although Dulha Rai's conquest of Dausa occurred between the late tenth and eleventh centuries, in order to fully elucidate his family background, there is a need to delve further back—all the way to the age of the Gupta Empire in north India.

The Gupta period is often hailed as the 'Golden Age' of Indian history, as it saw the flowering and crystallization of Indian culture in all aspects, be it art, science or literature. The end of the Gupta era marked the closing chapter of ancient India and the dawn of early medieval India. While the story of the Guptas, their decline and eventual fall, which was a result of several factors, are beyond the immediate scope of this book, some aspects are relevant to the history of Gopaksetra and eastern Rajasthan.

The End of the Gupta Era, but a Continuity in Culture

The fact is that while the position of the Imperial Guptas as the dominant power in north India disintegrated by the mid-sixth century, the legacy of high culture that germinated as a result of Gupta prosperity and progress did not simply vanish with the fall of the dynasty. It continued to thrive in the various successor states, albeit each with its own regional variations. There was, in fact, a semblance of continuity in terms of courtly culture, modes of warfare, coinage (numismatics), political ideology, which the post-Gupta period rulers and kingdoms inherited, as evident in their areas of dominance and cultural expression.

Take, for instance, mode of warfare. Troops were divided into regular troops (standing army) and irregular troops (auxiliary/tribal contingents). Forts were garrisoned by troops with garrison commanders who were loyal to the ruler. The main body of the army generally consisted of spearmen, while swords were of the straight-bladed Khanda type and were only used by those of high military status. The king and generals would be mounted on an armoured war elephant or war horses. And this remained so. North India, since time immemorial, has been known for its famed cavalry, and horse trade was a particularly robust and profitable trade in western India (particularly

Gujarat and Rajasthan), with horses being imported from central Asia, Arabia, Khurasan, although there were also domestic breeds such as the hardy Marwari (Malani) horse, the Kathiawari breed or the Tibetan pony found in the Himalayan regions. The use of the war chariot, which was popular during the Bronze Age, seems to have declined greatly by the early medieval era. These central units would be supported by auxiliaries such as archers, javelinmen, mace bearers, axemen, fighting ascetics or tribal units. The employment of mercenaries/part-time soldiers was also a strong feature of the Indian military market from the pre-Mauryan age up until the early nineteenth century.

The Guptas, unlike the Mauryas, did not centralize their rule but depended on the absorption or submission of the smaller rulers and feudatories of lesser kings (samatas) to the great kings (maharajas), who, in turn, owed their allegiance to the king of kings or emperors (maharajadhiraja/chakravarti), forming an offensive and defensive raja mandala (network of kings). As the historian R.C. Majumdar noted, 'once an enemy is conquered, the form in which he submits is immaterial; what matters is effective surrender. A victorious king should take care to destroy his enemies, but he should penalise only the wicked and the treacherous.' Further, he added:

> The learned and the pious of the conquered country should be honoured; restraints on the subjects should be removed; the poor and ailing should be treated with kindness; sports and rejoicing should be initiated. Justice and finance must be restored. Wise methods of

> governance should be introduced. Above all a policy of non-interference in the life of the people should be adopted.[1]

Central to the political system described was the principle of hereditary kingship, in which the king himself as the head of state was also the commander-in-chief of the armed forces. Sanskrit was the language of the court and the priests, while adherence to Vedic knowledge was the guiding principles of the realm.

A good king was meant to strictly follow the principles of *rajadharma* under the guidance of Dharma-sutras, chiefly *dandaniti* and the Arthashastra, among others. Nonetheless, it must be noted that the ruler's succession was not rigidly fixed, and while the eldest son often succeeded the father, it was not always the case. Succession disputes were also common if a clear line of succession was not established by the ruler before his death.

The royal court was not only the centre of administrative and cultural affairs but also the justice system. Royal princes were often appointed as governors of provinces as well as generals.[2] The king and the princes were advised by able mantris and purohits who, like the royal family, often (but not always) held the position in a heredity fashion. In fact, it is

[1]Majumdar, R.C. (ed.), 'Foreword', *The Age of Imperial Kanauj*, Bharatiya Vidya Bhavan, Bombay, p. 18.

[2]Terminologies used are: *rajanya* for the nobility, *rajasthaniya* for viceroys, *uparika* for governors, *amatya* for ministers and *dandapasika* for the police force. For the military titles, the general was known as the *dandanayaka*, the commander was the *baladhikrita*, while the commander of the fort was the *kottapala*.

believed that in the absence of more competent commanders, the senapatis were also expected to lead military campaigns if assigned to do so, with the purohit being the only one exempt, as he was needed by the king's side. These councils of mantris advised the king on matters relating to diplomatic relations, revenue, treasury, justice and so on.

Within this political system of inter-related alliances and relationships, a weaker state would seek an alliance of or protection of a more powerful ruler, and they, in turn, supported this greater sovereign in times of conflict, forming together into a warband, which was dismissed once the particular conflict was resolved. While the feudatory rulers governing autonomously in their own domain, they were bound to pay tribute to their overlord or supply him with a fixed quota of troops. In times of conflict or foreign invasion, they were also meant to join forces with their allies and overlord.

However, often when the former vassal became strong or saw an opportunity in the weakening of their former overlord, they broke free from him or established themselves as the new sovereign power in the land. Historian Daud Ali describes this political system of varying relationships between rulers of this period in detail:

> Paramount overlordship was typically established by a great military and diplomatic expedition called a 'conquest of the directions' or digvijaya, in which the ambitious king sought to defeat and/or gain the submission of neighbouring rulers, or to re-establish fallen or collateral lines, rather than expand the boundaries of his own territory. The Allahabad pillar

> inscription, praising the emperor Samudragupta's digvijaya, states that he defeated and reinstated a number of kings (grahana-moksanugraha, literally, 'capturing and releasing through favour') and re-established (pratishapana) fallen families. Imperial rule was constituted through the incorporation and re-articulation of separate and distinct lordships rather than the extension of boundaries of the land ruled directly by the emperor. The sources represent the paramount sovereign, not as the ruler of a realm, but as an 'enjoyer of the earth', for in this diplomatic language rulers of bounded realms were always lesser kings. The paramount sovereign gained the submission of such rulers, who were incorporated into his empire in the manner of fief-holding vassals.[3]

Instead of supporting him, their roles were now to contend with their old overlord until a clear result was formed or reconciliation was agreed upon by both parties, albeit a difference in the terms of relationship. Such conflicts shall be amply demonstrated in Chapter 3.

This policy of *grahana-moksha-anugraha* could be translated literally as:

> Grahana = capturing the enemy after defeating him in battle
>
> Moksha = liberation or releasing the enemy king after his defeat in battle

[3]Ali, Daud, *Courtly Culture and Political Life in Early Medieval India*, Cambridge University Press, 2004, p. 36.

Anugraha = the victor reinstates the enemy king as a ruler in his domain once again

The Gupta emperor Samudragupta is believed to have mastered the policy of *grahana-moksha-anugraha* in accordance to the nature and geographic location of the enemies he encountered. This is partly due to the near impossibility of retaining direct control over these distant subjugated regions. Thus, it was more pragmatic to be satisfied with the defeated rulers acknowledging his overlordship and becoming vassal-kings in a publicly recognized subsidiary alliance.

This policy of subsidiary alliance or indirect rule would be adopted by various powers, both imperial and regional, following the decline of the Imperial Guptas.[4]

Another notable social aspect of the early medieval period that makes it markedly different from the medieval period is the fact that the courtly women were not only highly educated but were often seen in public with the men and did not veil their faces, unlike the prevalent culture of the (later) medieval age[5], which continues to date in conservative communities. Additional information can be garnered from the fact that

---

[4]To put it in a more relatable manner, this could be seen as how the Rajput polities and states inherited this culture from earlier times, but on a scale limited mainly to north and central India due to the changes in South Asia's geopolitical landscapes. A relatable example is how the Thakurs, Rawals and Rais of Rajputana were considered an authority within their own domains, but it was to the maharaja of the state that they owed their allegiance and assisted in times of war or attended his court on special occasions, religious or otherwise.

[5]Majumdar refers to it as 'the age of resistance'.

Silamahadevi, wife of Dhruva, the famed Rashtrakuta ruler, was addressed as 'Paramesvari' or 'Paramabhattriki'. In other parts of India as well, courtly women were learned[6], and are believed to have acted as administrators on behalf of the king, examples being Sugandha and Didda of Kashmir, queens of the Kara dynasty in Orissa or Queen Prabhavati Gupta of the Vakataka dynasty.[7]

Foreign Trade and International Relations

Far from being isolated, India was a thriving centre of international trade and travel. Early medieval India was the land of Sanatana Dharma, and Indian science also reached its apogee under the Guptas, with universities like Nalanda and Vikramashila attracting students and scholars from all over the subcontinent and beyond.[8]

International trade with India had always been lucrative since at least the Bronze Age, and the early medieval period,

---

[6]In the words of R.C. Majumdar in reference to the courtly woman of the early medieval era, based on contemporary sources, 'Avantisundari, the wife of the poet Rajasekhara, was an exceptionally accomplished woman. The poet quotes her thrice in the Kavyamimamsa. His Karpuramanjari was produced at her request and Hemachandra quotes three of her Prakrit stanzas. Ubhayabharati or Sarasvati, wife of Mandanamisra, who acted as an arbitrator in her husband's disputations with Sankaracharya, was a learned scholar herself.' Majumdar, R.C. (ed.), 'Foreword', *The Age of Imperial Kanauj*, Bharatiya Vidya Bhavan, Bombay, 1955.

[7]Ibid. 19.

[8]The famed ancient university of Taxila (Takshashila), in present-day north western Pakistan, was, however, destroyed by the Huna invasion of the fourth century.

with which we are concerned, was no exception.

Indian traders, both in the form of maritime trade and caravans (land route), had varied kinds of trade and barter with neighbouring regions. In the north-west, Gujarat and its coastline was a contested region between different powers, as its ports enabled profitable trade between India and Persia, west Asia and beyond, following the old Roman trade route. In the east, the Bay of Bengal was of equal importance in spreading not only trade but also cultural exchanges between India and the Buddhist as well as Hindu kingdoms of Southeast Asia. The knowledge and culture that shone out from India was Arya Dharma, or the spreading of civilizations through Vedic, Brahmanical and Buddhist knowledge traditions and practices. It was the spreading of a higher consciousness that penetrated beyond the mundane and transient nature of the physical world and shone light upon the consciousness of nations and tribes across distant lands, uplifting their consciousness into an ascended state and a society based on the principal of Sanatana Dharma and dharmic rule. Although military conflicts were part and parcel of a king's duty, the timeless wisdom of Arya Dharma that emanated out of the Indian subcontinent lit up new cultures and kingdoms in far-off shores and distant peaks; it was not a mere tireless cycle of physical conquest and subjugation.

Throughout the long and turbulent history of the Sassanid Empire, its eastern border with India was mostly stable compared to its near constant conflict with the Byzantines to its west and the nomadic tribes to its north.[9] At

---

[9]Many tribes and kingdoms of central Asia were, in any case, people of

the early stages of Islam's inception, India was a fabled land far to the east, an ancient land famed for its war elephants and profitable trade in exotic spices, cloth, precious stones and other merchandise. Afghanistan and Kashmir also had prosperous Hindu as well as Buddhist kingdoms, which also acted as midway points that enabled cultural and commercial exchange between India and central Asia. Further north lay Tibet, China and the steppes beyond, all of whom had trade as well as cultural contact with India and regarded her as the sacred land of sages and kings.

By the early seventh century, as the Islamic Caliphate expanded (westwards in north Africa, and eastwards in Asia), its well-trained horsemen eventually reached the borders of the ancient Sassanid Empire, homeland of Zoroastrianism. Centuries of conflict with the Byzantine and other enemies had greatly drained the resources and military strength of the once-mighty Sassanids, whose rulers after the last great Shahanshah Khosrau II, rose and fell in rapid succession. Their vast domain was ripe for invasion by the faithful Arab steeds, a multi-generational process, which, despite the fall of the central authority at Ctesiphon, would still take over a century to complete.

During this period of Islam's early expansion, India was rightly viewed as an ancient civilization to the east of the Islamic world, and Arab traders were keen to trade with India (as their ancestors did since time immemorial). Indian rulers at the time, both coastal as well as inland, welcomed the early

Indo-European descent, thus, it was natural for them to maintain trade and cultural ties with 'mother' India.

Muslim traders, mostly Arab and Persian, fairly as they did all other foreign visitors, as attested by the ninth-century merchant Sulaiman or the chronicler Al-Masudi.

Additionally, it is through the records of these early Arab merchants and chroniclers, such as the tenth-century merchant Abu Said, that we have an attestation of the fact that queens indeed appeared alongside the kings at court, and the concept of purdah was unheard of and unnatural to India's ancient tradition.

Harshavardhana

Following the collapse of the Imperial Guptas, ancient states whose names were well-remembered at that time (but somewhat forgotten today) re-emerged and asserted their independence from the grip of Pataliputra, capital of Magadha and the imperial seat of power since the Mauryan age. As Magadha's power declined, other successor states resurfaced, such as Gauda (or Vanga) in Bengal, Valabhi in Gujarat, Kalinga in Odisha or Kamarupa in Assam. The important dynasties that emerged in the post-Gupta era, however, were based in two states that lay in the Gangetic plains—Pushyabhuti dynasty based in Sthaneshwar (present-day Thanesar in Ambala district, Punjab) and the Maukhari dynasty based in Kanyakubja of ancient India, better known today as the perfume city of Kannauj.

Historian Burjor Avari has suggested that the decline and eventual fall of the Guptas was a severe setback to the mode of imperial rule in north India, which was built up from the time of great rulers of the past, starting from the great

Chandragupta Maurya, Ashoka, Kanishka and the Gupta's own conqueror Samudragupta the Great. As opposed to the Gupta hegemony, the centuries following the mid-sixth century would be the age of competing regional kingdoms. These Gupta successor states and former feudatories would fight against as well as cooperate amongst one another. Various rulers with great ambitions and resources to match still dreamed of becoming a pan-India ruler or chakravarti, and this objective was indeed achieved in the seventh century by the abled Pushyabhuti ruler Harshavardhana. As the power of Pataliputra began to fade, and over 500 years before the rise of Delhi, Kannauj would become the most powerful city in north India as a centre of unimaginable wealth, power and high culture.

Despite the strong matrimonial alliance between the Pushyabhutis and the Maukharis, Rajyavardhana, the elder brother of Harshavardhana, waged war with both Shashanka, the king of Bengal to the east, and Devagupta, the ruler of Malwa in the south-west. This pattern of tripartite struggle with Kannauj at the centre stage would continue in some form or the other over the next five centuries in north India, as shall be expounded upon in the following chapters.

Harshavardhana, although the younger brother of the Maharaja Rajyavardhana, was, as though by divine grace, raised to become the ruler of both the Pushyabhutis and the Maukharis. When his brother was killed through trickery by Shashanka, the King of Gauda (Bengal)[10], Harshavardhana

[10]Avari, Burjor, *India: The Ancient Past: A History of the Indian Sub-continent from c.7000 BC to AD 1200*, Routledge, 2007, p. 183.

ascended the throne and subsequently gained control of much of the territory formerly held by the Imperial Guptas. The story of his dynasty and the conflicts that led to his enthronement is narrated by his court poet Banabhatta (popularly known Bana) in his famous Sanskrit composition *The Harshacharita*.

Having thus united the two great kingdoms of the Gangetic plain, he then went on to secure further spectacular victories, gaining submission of Kalinga and Kamarupa in the east, to Sindh as well as Valabhi in the west. Northwards, his influence was felt as far as Kashmir, while the Narmada was the southern border of his empire. Like most enlightened and cosmopolitan rulers of his age, he promoted and practised both Hinduism (particularly Shaivism) and Buddhism, a fact attested by the famous translator of sutras and pilgrim Chinese monk Xuanzang. Although no traces from the time of Harshavardhana remains, great Vedic and Buddhist rituals were said to have been performed on the riverbank of Kannauj, through which the Holy Ganga flowed.

The emperor Harshavardhana died without a clear successor in 648 CE, which naturally led to a period of chaos and disruption. The aftermath of his death resulted in a scenario witnessed repeatedly in the annals of human history in which the disintegration of a centralized power gives way to competition driven by the aspiration of successor states. The backdrop of the three centuries following the mid-eighth century until the beginning of the eleventh century in north India is best described as India's period of 'Tripartite' struggle for power, somewhat comparable to the Triumvirate period of the Roman Empire, or the

Three Kingdom period of Chinese history. Although there was a periodic change in the factions involved, the cause of disagreement would, more often than not, be his famed capital Kannauj. The control of Kannauj, with its strategic location almost at the centre of north India, enabled the power that held the city to dominate the Gangetic plains and threaten enemies in all directions.

Following the demise of Harshavardhana's empire, three main factions rose to become the major contenders of imperial power in north India—the Pratiharas of Rajasthan, the Rashtrakutas of the Deccan and the powerful Buddhist Pala kingdom of Bihar/Bengal. Of great significance is also the fact that the downfall of the Imperial Guptas and Harshavardhana led to the emergence of a new Kshatriya title of north India, leading to the beginning of the age of the Rajputs in north India. Although it was glorious while it lasted, Harshavardhana's reign was short-lived in comparison to some of the successor states that were to follow and attempt to imitate and even outdo the splendour in his court at Kannauj.

Rise of the Rajput Clans

According to B.D. Chattopadhyaya, who has researched extensively on the origin and history of the Rajputs, the emergence of these clans in the early medieval period was a widespread phenomenon of the proliferation of lineage-based states in north India.[11] Upinder Singh, another prominent

[11]Chattopadhya, B.D., *The Making of Early Medieval India*, Oxford University Press, New Delhi, 2012.

historian, points out a number of important factors such as the expansion of the agrarian economy, emerging features in land distribution among royal clansmen or temples, as well as widespread inter-clan collaboration in which political alliances were often sealed with a matrimonial alliance.[12]

While it is difficult to factually pin down the origins of the Rajputs as a race, without proper foray into genetics/DNA science, it could be said that it is more important to recognize them as the inheritors of the post-Harshavardhana's polity of northern India. Thus, from the transition of the Gupta period to the age in which Rajput clan-based states emerged, it was certainly not the case that all the old players in north Indian political circles disappeared. Rather, what transpired was that as the main players at the top vanished from the scene, it was now time for those previously in a subsidiary position to emerge and compete for power.

Indeed, there was also the emergence of pastoral tribes, who, over time, settled into a sedentary and agrarian lifestyle. As the settlement of the tribe grew, along with it grew the role of the tribe's leader as protector of not only the tribe but of cattle as well as Brahmins, an essential role of the Kshatriyas since the Vedic times. The Pratiharas, who rose to power from the eighth century onwards, seem to be a premier example of such a pastoral tribe whose leader became sedentary and achieved Kshatriya status of imperial proportions, a fact that was not realized by James Tod and shall be a subject of great

[12]Singh, Upinder, *History of Ancient and Early India: From the Stone Age to the 12th Century*, Pearson Education, 2008.

relevance to the topic at hand.[13]

It also warrants recognition that there was a pattern of martial culture in pastoral groups such as Jats, Gujjars, Bhils or Meenas, among others, who predated the 'new Rajput Great Tradition', which fully crystalized as a lineage-based Rajput identity in sixteenth-century Rajasthan. This implies that prior to 'new Rajput Great Tradition' and up until the early nineteenth century, there existed a persistent culture in which martial pastoralist tribes at times took up military service as a seasonal employment.[14] This gave India a unique position among the nations of the world of being a land with an unusually large supply of armed men in the military-labour market, which was not solely based on kin or religion of the employer (warlord).

Dutch historian Dirk H.A. Kolff reasonably argues that there was some measure of fluidity in the manner in which the tradition of armed peasantry and the military-labour market (through part-time soldiering) 'was a major generator of socio-religious identities'.[15]

---

[13]While to this date there are some members of the Parihar Rajputs (as they are known today) in Rajasthan, Madhya Pradesh and Uttar Pradesh, they have long been separated both from their glorious imperial past as well as their Gujjar brethren, who, till date, form a vital part of the populace in Rajasthan, Gujarat and other north Indian states. A large number of the Gujjars still adhere to their pastoral past as their ancestors did since time immemorial.

[14]A typical pattern would be a year traveling in the military service of a warband, after which they would return to cultivate their fields and spend time in their native villages.

[15]Kolff further states, 'There was no lack of men opting for a life spent as errant soldier, migrant labourer or pack animal trader. Perhaps the meaning of Rajput, in this context, is not properly conveyed by the literal translation of

Therefore, it could be argued that what became known as Rajput is the combination of both ancient Kshatriya lineages, which were able to resurface and compete for power after the decline of Harshavardhana's empire, as well as the emergence of pastoral tribes that, over the centuries, gained landed status as local gentries, be it Thakurs, Rawals or Rai (as well as zamindaris in the medieval period). To label them exclusively as one or the other would be presumptuous. The fact that the lineage or kula is acknowledged as being divided into Solar (Suryavanshi), Lunar (Chandravanshi), Naga (Nagavanshi) and Fire (Agnikula), in itself points out to the differing ancestral origins. In this context, it is better to understand the Rajputs not as a single race but as a cognitive term for the north Indian Kshatriyas of the present age, whose domain is to be found in the aridness of the great Thar, stretching into the Himalayan hills as well as the Gangetic doab and beyond.

An interesting note on some of the achievements of the Rajputs is given by William Barton. He says:

> The Rajputs may claim to have saved Hinduism in the north. That is their chief title to renown. Almost equally important is their gift to India of the most enduring of her political institutions, the Rajput State. Let us for a moment examine the structure of this institution. The

---

'son of king'; it is also the proud name of all adventuring young men or Jawans, in search of a truly paternal and kingly patron. Historically, such men were far more numerous than the members of the successful aristocratic lineages of north India.' Kolff, D.H.A., *Naukar Rajput and Sepoy: The Ethnohistory of the Military Labour Market in Hindustan, 1450–1850,* Cambridge University Press, 2002, p. 74.

> basis is feudal. The King or Maharaja is the supreme authority as head of the clan or group of families that originally settled on the soil. The associated families are represented by barons or Thakurs holding on a service tenure: under them are minor landowners down to the smallest unit, the holder of which was responsible for producing a single horseman for the feudal levy. The nobles have the right to advice the ruler: in the old days they frequently elected a new sovereign when the direct heir was unfitted to succeed.[16]

The Different Rajput Vanshis

The most powerful of the early Rajput states following the downfall of Harshavardhana's empire were the states belonging to the Agnikula (fire-born) Pratiharas, the Chalukyas, the Paramaras and the Chauhans (Chahamanas). According to a legend that alludes to the origin of these Agnivanshi clans:

> In ancient times the Brahmans were sorely persecuted by the demons, who in spite of the sanctity of mount Abu, desecrated their shrines, extinguished the sacrificial flames and rendered their offerings impure. The harassed Rishis persevered, however and reassembling round the Agnipkunda rekindled the sacred fire and prayed to Mahadeva for assistance. The god at once gave ear to their supplications and there issued from the flames a figure of peaceful mien whom the Brahmans appointed

[16] Barton, William, *The Princes of India*, Nisbet & Co., 1934, p. 93.

> guardian of the gate, hence his name of Prithi-ka-dwara or Parihara, 'earth's door'. After fresh invocations to the gods, a second figure came out of the fire, and being formed in the Chalu, or palm of the hand was called Chalukya. A third figure appeared in the same manner who was called Pramara or 'first striker' as he was the first to go forth against the demons, who however proved too strong for him. At the fourth incantation a terrible figure emerged from the fire, lofty in stature, fierce in aspect, clad in armour and four armed, hence his name Chauhan. Fortified with the blessings of the Brahmans, the latter was again despatched against the powers of darkness, and this time prevailed. He slew their leaders and pursued the vanquished demons to the nethermost depths of hell.[17]

This legend pertaining to the inception of the Agnivanshis is inevitably linked to the sacred Mount Abu, which James Tod rightly describes as the 'Mount Olympus of Rajputana'. Moreover, it seems to indicate a great ritualistic absolution or purification ceremony of four great tribes that may have included former invaders, such as remnants of the Kushans, Scythians or Hunas, into the Hindu Kshatriya fold. Thus, Mount Abu and its myriad mystery is said to be the firepit from which the Agnivanshi Rajputs sprang forth.[18]

A.H. Bingley concurs with this view regarding the legend pertaining the mythical origin of the Agnikula and

---

[17]Bingley, A.H., *Handbook on Rajputs*, Asian Educational Services, New Delhi, 1986, pp. 110–11.

[18]This view is also supported by Alf Hiltebeitel.

comments on the possibility that the legend may indicate the fact that Scythian mercenaries/tribes 'obtained recognition as Kshatriyas as a reward for their services to Hinduism'.[19]

There are, however, overcomplicated issues concerning the older acknowledged Lunar, Solar and Naga lineages of other Kshatriya tribes, which are matters that go far beyond the immediate concerns of this book, into the realms of mythological understanding and antediluvian polities. Professor Dasharatha Sharma, eminent historian of Rajasthani history, rightly comments that whatever were the origins of these clans, be it Indian or foreign, Brahminical or Kshatriya, they were, by the eighth century, regarded as Kshatriyas who shouldered the Kshatriya ethics and duty of defending the land, its people and culture.[20]

Therefore, despite their differing origins, centuries of intermarriage had, by the fourteenth century, forged them closer genetically and culturally into an analogous Rajput polity and etiquette.

With regards to the Rajput clans of early medieval Rajasthan specifically, Dasharatha Sharma opines that the most important were the Pratiharas of Maru and Gurjaradesha, Mauryas of Chittor and Kota, the Guhilas of Mewar, the Chapas as well as Chauhans and Naga rulers.

Although, today, the Gurjara-Pratihara dynasty find little mention outside of medieval history classes, they are a subject of immense relevance to the investigation at hand.

---

[19]Bingley, A.H., *Handbook on Rajputs*, Asian Educational Services, New Delhi, 1986, p. 111.

[20]Sharma, Dasharatha, *Rajasthan Through the Ages*, Vol. 1, Rajasthan State Archives, Bikaner, 1966, p. 106.

It is believed that the Gujjar tribe, which gave its name to Gujarat, made up the population of this dynasty, while the Pratiharas were the royal branch, although their name is literally translated as 'gatekeeper' or perhaps 'guardian' (of the temple).

It must be noted that the Arabs who had made a foothold in Sindh in the early eighth century and attempted to expand westwards into Rajasthan and Gujarat were halted on their tracks by the contingents of the early Pratihara ruler Nagabhata I. Thus having contained the Arab's attempted expansion, the subsequent two centuries would be the period of glory and suzerainty for the Pratiharas until the demise of their last powerful king, Vinayakapala of Kannauj, in around 943 CE. Vinayakapala's death was followed by a succession dispute, which ensued for many years and greatly contributed to the Pratiharas' overstretched domain being overtaken by the most powerful of their former subsidiary allies. First among these was the Chauhans, who themselves became a great force to be reckoned with in north-west India; this was also the time during which Chitrakuta (Chittor) was taken from the Pratiharas by the Guhila ruler Bhartrapatta II.[21] Amid this backdrop was also the competing interests and rising power of the Chandelas, Tomars and the Kachaphaghatas (in central India). A number of families survived as well as evolved through the fury of the age and became the great clans that dominated the politics of late medieval Rajasthan and established their names as some of the greatest kingdoms of the desert state. The Sisodias of Mewar claim descent to

[21]Hooja, Rima, *A History of Rajasthan*, Rupa & Co., New Delhi, 2006, p. 190.

their august ancestor Bappa Rawal of the Guhila clan, while the Rathores of Marwar claim descent from the Rashtrakutas of the Deccan, who on several occasions between the ninth and tenth centuries, became the conquerors of Kannauj.

Prior to the migration of the Kachwahas across the Chambal River and the establishment of Dausa as their first capital (in Rajasthan), the dynasty was associated with the Kachaphaghatas, a faction that ruled over the forgotten domain of Gopaksetra in the north-western region of the modern state of Madhya Pradesh and portions of Uttar Pradesh.

TWO

GOPAKSETRA AND THE RISE OF THE KACHAPHAGHATAS

The lack of clarification with regards to Dulha Rai's exact origin prior to his establishing Dausa as the first capital of Dhundhar has been noted by many historians. Many sources mention that he was from Gwalior, while some others state that he was from Narwar. Upon better examination, however, one finds that these statements are by no means contradictory, for they merely indicate that he was a scion of the (early medieval) dynasty known to historians as the Kachaphaghatas. Both Gwalior and Narwar are, in fact, known to have been Kachaphaghata strongholds from the mid-tenth century till sometime in the twelfth century. I, however, believe that their association to the area precedes these dates by many centuries.

Dulha Rai is often described as an adventurer who emerged and founded the kingdom of Dhundhar by chance.

His Kachaphaghata background and connection is, however, rarely mentioned or analysed.

On the other hand, the general consensus of historians who accept Dulha Rai's Kachaphaghata ancestry/connection is that he conquered Dausa after his marriage to a Chauhan princess, whose name is recorded as Sojan Kumari in the genealogical records of the Kachwahas. It was this matrimonial alliance that enabled him to oust the Badgurjars, who along with the Chauhans were the previous lords of Dausa. This chapter points out facts and clues with regards to Dulha Rai's ancestral domain of Gopaksetra based on available information as well as an open/intuitive perspective to history.

History of Gopaksetra

Historian David Henige notes in *Princely States of India*, that 'Jaipur was one of the major Rajput states and its ruler was acknowledged as the head of the Kachwaha Rajputs, who claim descent from Rama through the medieval Kachchhapaghata dynasty.'[22]

In order to tackle the issue of Dulha Rai's ancestry, we shall first evaluate some information available relating to the homeland of early medieval Kachaphaghata dynasty. All sources agree that Kachaphaghatas were known chiefly as the rulers of Simphaniya (Sihonia), Gopagiri (Gwalior), Kuntalpur (Kutwar), Nalapura (Narwar), Dubkund and the surrounding ravines of the Chambal region, known in ancient

[22]Henige, David, *Princely States of India: A Guide to Chronology and Rulers*, Orchid Press, Bangkok, 2004, p. 76.

times as Gopaksetra, corresponding to the modern districts of Gwalior, Morena, Bhind, Shivpuri and parts of Guna and Datia districts of Madhya Pradesh, and the district of Jhansi in present-day Uttar Pradesh.

Gopaksetra was a land surrounded by rivers on three sides. Specifically, it was the area that lay east of the Chambal River (known in ancient times as Charmanvati). The Yamuna River formed the northern boundary of Gopaksetra, and the Betwa River lay in its west. Michael D. Willis further points out that for those approaching from the north or west, the Chambal River acted as a natural barrier;[23] it may be said that the Chambal River turned Gopaksetra into a cul-de-sac. The Chambal region has always acted as a formidable buffer that discouraged both potential invaders as well as travellers who tended to bypass the northern part of this region rather than attempting to cross it. The Chambal region was and still is a wild riverine realm of aquatic creatures and prehistoric reptiles such as the gharial (*Gavialis gangeticus*), the mugger crocodile (*Crocodylus palustris*; an added danger to outsiders attempting to pass through), tortoises, turtles of varied species and even the Ganges river dolphin. Some of these species, however, are currently facing challenges to their survival due to the unsustainable management of the river in recent decades.

It is interesting to note that these geographical features rendered Gopaksetra a strategically blessed landscape for

[23]Willis, Michael D., 'An introduction to the Historical Geography of Gopaksetra, Dasarna and Jejakadesa', *Bulletin of the School of Oriental and African Studies*, vol. 51, no. 2 (1988).

a ruling Kshatriya lineage—the fact that its western and northern boundaries were protected by the Chambal River, while the Sind as well as the Betwa rivers to the east also made it easily defendable. The only serious threat faced by Gopaksetra would be a large and well-organized invasion from the south, which was certainly not a regular occurrence in history, although the advent of time and ravages of war spares none, as shall be explored.

Gopaksetra was surrounded by three ancient regions—Jejakabhukti (Bundelkhand) situated to its east, ancient Dasarna to its south and Malava/Avanti (Malwa) lay to its west. Across the Chambal River to its west was the ancient state of Virata (Bairat in the Jaipur district of Rajasthan), and to its north in eastern Rajasthan/western Uttar Pradesh were the kingdoms of Surasena (Braj region) and famed Matsyadesha (Alwar, Karauli and south-eastern side of Jaipur). Among the earliest important settlements around Gopaksetra was Padmavati (Pawaya), the former capital of the Naga rulers for over three centuries (first to third centuries CE). According to M.B. Garde, the superintendent of archaeology for Gwalior State, Padmavati and Kutwar were, in the third century, capitals of the Naga rulers, which find mention in the Vishnu Purana. A vivid description of the city was given by Bhavbhuti in his renowned play titled 'Malati Madhava', which was based in Padmavati. The place even appears to have had a university that attracted students from far and wide. Archaeological artefacts such as coins, brick foundations and other relics from the early centuries of the Christian Era have been discovered in these vicinities.[24]

Padmavati would, through the chaos and warfare of the late third to fifth centuries, eventually be overshadowed by the growth of strategically important Gwalior and Narwar, both cities that have undeniable links to the Kachaphaghatas.

There were numerous other ancient sites in the region, such as Nalesvara (Naresar), Padhavali (Paroli), while to the south of Gopaksetra stood Rannod and the nearby archaeological sites of Surwaya (ancient Aarasvatipattana), Terahi (ancient Terami) and the temple town of Kadwaha (ancient Kadambaguha).[25]

The Naga strongholds of this period also include Vidisha and Kantipuri; however, the most important city was most certainly Padmavati (with its nine recorded Naga rulers). Mathura in ancient Surasena was yet another cosmopolitan centre of the Nagas during this period.

Gopaksetra and the Guptas

This golden age of Naga rule in Padmavati coincides with the rise of the neighbouring Gupta Empire under the first Gupta emperor Chandragupta I (r. 335–336 CE). Matters, however, turned grim for the Nagas with the ascendance of Samudragupta (r. 336–375 CE), the successor of Chandragupta I who rose to power after defeating a rival

---

[24]Garde, M.B., *Archaeology in Gwalior*, Department of Archaeology, Gwalior State, 1924, p. 9.

[25]Willis, Michael D., 'An introduction to the Historical Geography of Gopaksetra, Dasarna and Jejakadesa', *Bulletin of the School of Oriental and African Studies,* vol. 51, no. 2 (1988), pp. 271–78.

curiously named Kachagupta.

Samudragupta continued his father's expansionist policy and firmly planted Gupta suzerainty beyond the confines of north India. His exploits and far-reaching conquests are recorded in the iconic Prayag Prashasti (also widely known as the Allahabad Pillar Inscription).

In reference to the Nagas of Gopaksetra, Tej Ram Sharma states that they were mighty rulers who had performed no less than 10 Vedic Ashvamedha sacrifices and their power lasted for a lengthy period spanning centuries. Having been natives of the region prior to the time of the Kushan Empire, they managed to hold on to power until the ascension of Samudragupta the Great. The name of Ganapatinaga as well as that of other Naga kings was found listed as kings who were defeated by Samudragupta, as recorded in the Prayag Prashasti.[26]

According to the Prayag Prashasti, Samudragupta's opponents were divided into four categories.[27] First were slain rulers, whose dominions were outright annexed by the emperor. Second were the frontier kings who were forced to pay homage to Samudragupta. Third were rulers who were defeated and then reinstated under a subsidiary alliance. Lastly, were distant kings who acknowledged Samudragupta as emperor by sending him diplomatic embassies (and most likely trade missions). Samudragupta adopted a different policy towards different enemies he encountered. In the

---

[26]Sharma, Tej Ram, *A Political History of the Imperial Guptas: From Gupta to Skandagupta*, Concept Publishing Company, Delhi, 1989, p. 24.
[27]Ibid.

Ganga–Yamuna Doab region, he followed the first policy of annexation, in which nine Naga rulers were defeated and their lands incorporated under direct Gupta administration. The second category consisted of neighbouring frontier states, both kingdoms as well as republican states of Punjab and western India, who agreed to pay tribute and taxes to the Gupta Empire while they remained nominally independent. In the third category was included *atavika rajya*s, or the forest kingdoms of central India, that were said to be defeated and their rulers reinstated as feudatory rulers under Gupta suzerainty. Under the fourth category were other neighbouring nations, such as Sri Lanka or Kashmir, who exchanged diplomatic embassies and trade missions with the Gupta Empire.

Thus, despite their strength, the coalition of Naga kings, due to their proximity to the Gupta heartland of western Matsyadesha and Magadha, were deemed to be a sufficient threat, which led to the Naga capitals of Mathura and Padmavati being directly annexed by the armies of Samudragupta. Nonetheless, it is not beyond the realm of possibility that smaller pockets of Naga rulers subsisted, as they may have been deemed insignificant to cause trouble or may have submitted their allegiance to the rising Gupta power and did not pose a threat to them, unlike the famed Naga rulers of Padmavati and Mathura. As a matter of fact, Samudragupta's son, Chandragupta II, is recorded as having married a Naga princess.[28] This was perhaps a measure to appease the

[28]Avari, Burjor, *India: The Ancient Past: A History of the Indian Sub-continent from c. 7000 BC to AD 1200*, Routledge, 2007, p. 158.

surviving remnants of the archaic Naga confederacy in north India, which was vital to the maintenance of peace within the burgeoning Gupta Empire. It has been known that Naga states were still in existence during the mid-sixth century, as evident from the inscription of Nagavarman (after the fall of the Gupta Empire), which demonstrates that Naga influence, though much diminished, endured in some form or the other (both monarchic and republican).[29] This is partly owing to the sheer inaccessibility of the Naga domains in Rajasthan as well as the pristine wilderness of the Chambal region, a view that is also suggested by Ahmed Ali.[30]

Most notably, it is this period of Padmavati's decline that inevitably led to its importance being overshadowed by Gopagiri, which turned out to be a pivotal chapter in the emergence of the Kachaphaghatas.

The Huna Invasion and Disintegration of the Gupta Empire

Having administered Gopaksetra for nearly two centuries, by the mid-fifth century, the Guptas themselves faced a mortal threat in the form of the Hephthalite or Huna invasion from the north-western frontier. This threat was temporarily halted by the victory of the great Gupta emperor Skandagupta (r. 455–467 CE) over the Huna hordes, which checked their advance into India for over three decades.

[29]Willis, Michael D., *Inscriptions of Gopaksetra: Materials for the History of Central India*, British Museum Press, 1996, p. 111.

[30]Ali, Ahmed, *Kachchhapaghata Art and Architecture*, Publication Scheme, Jaipur, 2005.

But by the beginning of the sixth century, the invaders[31] returned and having ransacked much of Sasanian Persia and capturing Gandhara, they renewed their attack into the Gupta Empire under their famed leader Toramana (r. 490–515 CE). The death of emperor Budhagupta in 495 CE marked the beginning of the end for the Imperial Guptas. In eastern Malwa, their rule practically ended while disorder and confusion reigned the day. Taking advantage of this internal conflict were the Hunas, whose advance must have seemed apocalyptic to the inhabitants of villages and towns that witnessed Toramana's horsemen as they conquered Kashmir, Punjab, parts of northern Rajasthan, eastern Malwa and briefly threatened the Gupta heartland of Magadha.

As a result of the Hunic invasion of Malwa, Gopaksetra is also believed to have been, for a short period, under the control of Toramana's son Mihirakula[32], the last Huna king of India in the first quarter of the sixth century, based on an inscription in Gwalior Fort, dated 525 CE.[33] The cruel Hunic dominance was short-lived, as the Hunas were expelled from central and north India by a coalition of local rulers led by the legendary Yashodharman of the Aulikara dynasty of Malwa and the Gupta ruler Narasimhagupta Baladitya. According to K.C. Jain, 'the defeats of Mihirakula by Baladitya and Yasodharman were two different events

[31]This wave of Hunic invaders are referred to as the Alkhon Huns.

[32]Began his reign in 515 CE, but the end of his reign seems to be a matter of debate.

[33]Willis, Michael D., *Inscriptions of Gopaksetra: Materials for the History of Central India*, British Museum Press, 1996, p. 19.

which were not synchronous. According to B.P. Singh, the victory of Baladitya may be put in 520 AD, while the success of Yasodharman over Mihirakula should be placed in, or shortly before, 533 AD.'[34]

Having defeated the forces of Mihirakula and freeing central and northern India from the Hunas, Yashodharman became the leading power of north India, temporarily even eclipsing the Guptas. There are, at Sondhi near Mandsaur (Mandasor), two great monoliths/pillars that have been attributed to King Yashodharman,[35] erected to commemorate his great victory over the Hunas. German orientalist Max Muller even believes that he was responsible for the wide spread and adaptation of the Vikram Samvat calender.[36] While he is still regarded as a legendry king of Malwa, his great prestige and majesty only lasted as long as he was alive. Yashodharman of Malwa rose to fulfil his dharmic duty from 530 to 540 CE, defeating foreign invaders and re-establishing a semblance of order across the land, which must have been greatly appreciated by the people of differing kingdoms and states that were reeling from the aftereffects of decades of war and invasions. K.C. Jain notes that upon the death of Yashodharman, his empire perished with him, and as consequence of it, this period was marked by the rise of several powerful feudatory principalities of the former Gupta Empire.[37]

---

[34]Jain, K.C., *Malwa Through The Ages*, Motilal Banarasidass, New Delhi, 1972, pp. 249–50.

[35]Known as the Mandasor Pillar Inscriptions of Yashodharman.

[36]However credit for its creation is mostly given to Chandragupta II, who adopted the name Vikramaditya.

[37]Jain, K.C., *Malwa Through The Ages*, Motilal Banarasidass, New Delhi, 1972, p. 259.

Admittedly, the immediate history of Gopaksetra following the ousting of the Hunas and the disintegration of the Gupta Empire is murky. A point agreed upon even by a specialist such as Michael D. Willis, who states that in the second half of the seventh century there was no centralized power in north India, as the later Guptas were confined to the heartland of Magadha in Bihar, while the Mauryas of Mathura ruled western Madhyadesha (in Rajasthan and UP). Gopaksetra and its vicinity were divided into a number of principalities. Willis comments on the state of Gopaksetra and neighbouring lands south of the Yamuna quoting Taranatha's description of the country during this period: 'Every Ksatriya, Brahmana and merchant was a king in his own area, but there was no king ruling over the country.'[38]

The next inscription of note to be found in Gopaksetra is that which belonged to Nagavarman, who, according to Willis, 'seems to have been an independent ruler in the mid-sixth century.'[39] It would appear that following the ousting of the Hunic invaders (as they did with the Kushans), control of the area reverted to the local chieftains, being as the name indicates, a Naga ruler.

Remnants of Naga power as demonstrated above survived not only the onslaught of Samudragupta[40] but also the Hephthalite (Huna) annexation of Gwalior under Mihirakula, for the landscape of Chambal and the geographic features of Gopaksetra was treacherous. Invaders were allowed to

[38]Willis, Michael D., *Temples of Gopakṣetra: A Regional History of Architecture and Sculpture in Central India AD 600–900,* British Museum Press, 1997, p. 19.
[39]Ibid.
[40]See Appendix I.

occupy the main roadways and the fortified townships, while the ravines and waterways of Gopaksetra would have been in the control of local chieftains.

It would seem logical that after ousting the foreign invading Hunas, Naga rulers would re-emerge to capture the towns and castles previously occupied by enemy forces and begin the arduous task of rebuilding their home ground from the embers of war and foreign occupation.

It was from this period that Padmavati's power waned, diminished in glory after the annexation by the Imperial Guptas as well as the torch and arrows of the Hunas. By the eleventh century, Padmavati was eclipsed by settlements such as Sihonia and Narwar, while Gwalior, founded by the young local Kachaphaghata ruler Suryasena, also Suraj Sen or Suraj Pal, in eighth century CE, had, by then, for many centuries been the principal city of Gopaksetra.

It is not beyond the realm of possibility that the Kachaphaghatas were a solar-worshipping branch or a ruling branch/faction related to the Nagas of Gopaksetra.

The rising importance of Gwalior and Narwar as the major settlements by the sixth century CE and the gradual eclipse of Padmavati in the region lend credit to this hypothesis. At any rate, it is safe to say that from the fourth to the sixth centuries, the dominance of the Nagas in Gopaksetra declined initially due to their conflict with the Imperial Guptas followed by the trail of destruction left behind by the Hunas. The influence and power of the Nagas in the area was gradually but undeniably supplanted by that of the Kachaphaghatas.

The Founding of Gwalior and the Rise of the Kachaphaghatas

In his book *The Rajput Palaces*, Giles Tillotson states that the citadel of Gwalior had become a settlement since around the sixth century, and certainly at least from the tenth century, for in about 950 CE, a Hindu dynasty was founded there by Suraj Pal. When this became extinct in 1129, it was followed by the Parihara dynasty.[41]

The Hindu dynasty referred by Tillotson is none other than the Kachaphaghata dynasty. In local history of Madhya Pradesh, it is affirmed that Gwalior was founded and, alongside Narwar, ruled by the Kachwahas. The legend of Suraj Sen and the Sage Gwalipa is enshrined in the local history of the area and documented by several sources.

Although the origins of Narwar as a settlement and its association with the epic of Raja Nala appears to be a matter of even greater mystery and antiquity (as shall be briefly examined in Chapter 4), it is irrefutable that Narwar came to be closely associated with the Kachaphaghatas after the decline of Naga power in the area. This view is supported by archaeologist Alexander Cunningham's statement that in 275 CE, they established their capital at Narwar and were classically known as Naisadha.[42]

In the *History of the Fortress of Gwalior*, by Shrimant

---

[41]Tillotson, Giles, *The Rajput Palaces: The Development of an Architectural Style, 1450–1750*, Oxford University Press, 1999, p. 56.

[42]Cunningham, A., *Archaeological Survey of India Report*, Vol. 1, 1871, pp. 56, 106–07, 161–62; Ray, H.C., *The Dynastic History of Northern India: Early Medieval Period*, Vol. II, Munshiram Manoharlal, New Delhi, 1973, pp. 821–22.

Balwant Row Bhayasaheb Scindia, the earliest account of the founding of Gwalior is related in great details:[43]

> Later researches, made subsequent to the downfall of the Mughul dynasty and the advent of the British in India connect the foundation of this stupendous structure in the third century after Christ (275 AD) with a memorable incident in the life of a Kutchwaha Thakur named Suraj Sen, who...suddenly became the progenitor of a royal race well-known in the annals of Gwalior.

According to Scindia's account, Suraj Sen, the thakur of Sehonia, was afflicted with leprosy for a period of two years. One day, while on a hunting expedition, thirsty and faint with exhaustion, he reached the spot where the Gawlior Fort stands today. It was a desolate rocky landscape. Suddenly, a Hindu ascetic appeared in front of him, who offered him a coarse handkerchief to procure water from a nearby spring for both of them. The Thakur strictly obeyed the mystic's orders. The ascetic, after tasting the water offered some to the thirsty traveller. The sadhu then expressed sympathy for the thakur's disease and advised him to bathe in the spring on a Sunday, which happened to be the next day, fortunately.

The next day, the Thakur went back to the spring with his whole family and retinue of villagers, and bathed in it to find himself immediately cured. Overjoyed at his recovery, the Thakur then fell at the feet of the ascetic in gratitude. The sadhu blessed the Thakur and suggested him to widen the bed of the spring and lay the foundation of a 'pucca' fort at

[43]Scindia, B.R.B., *History of the Fortress of Gwalior*, Bombay, 1892.

the same site, proclaiming that the fort would be the seat of a long line of kings from the Thakur's own family and that the family take the name 'Pal'. When the Thakur expressed his concerns of undertaking such a humongous effort due to limited resources, the sage offered him a batua 'containing a few pieces of metal and flints', which he assured would be enough to raise the fort. Then, 'Calling Suraj Sen then by the name of Suraj Pal, and placing the palm of his holy hand on the head of the newly created king, the hermit disappeared in an instant as if he never had any existence at all.'

With regards to the naming of the fort and subsequent township, the narrative continues:

> The name of the yogi, who lived simply on the vegetables of the forest, was 'Gwalpa Sidh' or the saint who received his illumination from his faith in the cowherds or playmates of the god Krishna...Suraj Sen ascended the guddee under the name Suraj Pal...

According to Scindia, the construction of the Gwalior Fort was completed during Suraj Pal's lifetime. The Suraj Kund was also built during his time. He reigned 36 years and died a natural death. He was succeeded by his son, Rasak Pal, who reigned only a year, and passed on the kingdom to his own son, Nahar Pal, who is credited with raising a temple dedicated to Lord Mahadeva or Shiva, which still stands.

In the opinion of Cunningham, considered by many to be the father of Indian archaeology and trusted translator of ancient inscriptions (and an enthusiastic numismatist), the Kachaphaghatas were known, according to bardic traditions, as having descended from Kusa (Kush), one of the two sons of the epic Dharma king Rama. According to bardic chronicles, after their migration out of Ayodhya of lore, the family first ruled from the fortress of Rohtas on the Sone River between Bihar and Bengal, and through the centuries, they are believed to have migrated westwards into Gopaksetra.

The legend pertaining to the founding of Gwalior fort is given as follows:

> The hill on which the fortress of Gwalior is situated was originally called Gopachal or Gopagiri. It was named Gwalior after a hermit Gwalipa who lived there. Cunningham thus relates the story: 'Gwalior was founded by a Kachwaha chief named Suraj Sen, the petty Raja of Kuntalpuri or Kutwar. Suraj Sen was a leper and one day while thirsty with hunting near the hill of Gopagiri, he came to the cave of Gwalipa and asked for water. The hermit gave him water in his own vessel and no sooner had he drunk it than he was cured from leprosy. The grateful Raja then asked what to do for the holy man and he was directed to build a fort on the hill; and the fort was called 'Gwali – awar' or Gwalior as it is written.'[44]

To this date, the pond (kund) from which the sage gave water to prince Suraj Sen is still in existence near Gwalior Fort and is known locally as the Suraj Kund, and, in fact,

---

[44]Monserrate, Antonio, *The Commentary of Father Monserrate S.J., on His Journey to the Court of Akbar*, translated by J.S. Hoyland, annotated by S. N. Banerjee, Asian Educational Services, New Delhi, 1922, p. 23.

predates the building of Gwalior as the founding legend indicates. That no other Rajput or Kshatriya clan can make this connection to the early history and founding of Gwalior is often ignored.

The scholar Ahmed Ali, who wrote a book titled *Kachchhapaghata Art and Architecture*, suggests that there is a link between the Nagas of Padmavati and the Kachaphaghatas. Whether this link was direct or through matrimonial alliance, we do not have any clear evidence, but several clues lie in the legend pertaining to the founding of Gwalior Fort by Suraj Sen as explored previously. The story emerges in the third century CE, a period which coincides with the decline of Padmavati, famed capital of the Naga rulers[45], and is inevitably linked to the rise of Gwalior and Narwar. According to Ahmed Ali:

> A. Cunningham and Gorelal Tiwari are of the opinion that the first ruler of this family was ruling over the area extending from Bharatpur, Dhaulpur to the western part of the Bundelkhand. These scholars have further suggested that Nala was the ancestor of the Naga kings, who were ruling over Padmavati, Kuntalapuri and Vidisha till fourth century AD, and they were lastly uprooted by Samudragupta. They further add that the first Kacchchhapaghata ruler was Suraja Sena, who ruled at Kuntalpuri and founded the fort of Gopadrigiri in the third century AD. Thus the Nagas and the Kachchhapaghatas have the common origin. It was when Samudragupta killed the rulers of Naga family,

[45]For further history of the Nagas, please see Appendix I.

> they were forced to leave this territory and sought the shelters in the forest, where they lived like Sudras and Nisadha—the hunters of fish and tortoise.[46]

The fact that the Kachaphaghatas ruled Narwar during the tenth and eleventh centuries is also supported by the 1120 AD (VS 1177) grant issued from Nala-pura-mahadurga by Vir Singh.[47] According to M.B. Garde:

> The history of the fortress of Narwar dates at least from the medieval times and is coupled with that of the brother fortress of Gwalior which is some 60 miles away. Both the forts passed through various vicissitudes and witnessed the rule of a number of Rajput dynasties. The more important of the Rajput dynasties which ruled over Narwar were Kachawahas, the Tomaras, and the Jajapellas.[48]

Thus, Raghubir Sinh of Sitamau, who edited the 1984 publication of Jadunath Sarkar's *A History of Jaipur* was mistaken in his assertion that 'Narwar first became associated with the Kachwaha house of Amber only during the reign of Akbar, when he gave Narwar in jagir to Raja Askaran Kachwaha, the dispossessed son of Raja Bhim and grandson of Raja Prithviraj of Amber.'[49]

With light now shed on to the history of the early medieval

---

[46]Ali, Ahmed, *Kachchhapaghata Art and Architecture*, Publication Scheme, Jairpur, 2005, p. 1.

[47]Cunningham, A., *Archaeological Survey of India Report*, Vol II, 1871, p. 313.

[48]Garde, M.B., *Archaeology in Gwalior*, Department of Archaeology, Gwalior State, 1924, pp. 105–06.

[49]Sarkar, Jadunath, *A History of Jaipur c. 1503-1938*, Raghubir Sinh (ed.), Orient Longman, 1984, p. 28.

Kachaphaghatas, it should be noted that Narwar Raj returned to Kachwaha rule with the aid of Akbar (after five centuries!), and Askaran's overlordship of Narwar is by no means the clan's 'first' association with this ancient fortress. According to Professor Bhatnagar, who penned *Life and Times of Sawai Jai Singh*: 'A synchronous study of the inscriptions of the Kacchaphagatas, the bardic traditions, and the genealogical tables, suggests that the Kachwahas of Amber and Gwalior had emanated from the Narwar house, which was the main stem.'[50]

The Tortoise and the Transformation in Name

Ahmed Ali's mention in his book that the family was for a while[51] forced to hunt tortoises for a living while dwelling in the pristine forest of early medieval India is rather fascinating. Now, it must be noted that apart from Narwar and Gwalior, other places that had a strong association with the Kachaphaghatas were Kutwar and Sihonia, where Suraj Sen is said to have originated from. This fact, at the very least, substantiates that there were known places where this family could seek refuge during difficult times. However, firstly, there are a number of precedents in (not only Indian) history in which ruling lineages were forced to take refuge in the hinterland of hills, forest and riverine terrains while their former capitols were occupied by a hostile force. Even the legendary Rana Pratap of Mewar was

---

[50]Bhatnagar, V.S., *Life and Times of Sawai Jai Singh 1688–1743*, Impex India Delhi, 1974, p. 3.

[51]After their defeat by Samudragupta.

forced to live with his family in the forests of Chavand, from where he continued his guerrilla warfare against his enemies, following the fall of Khumbalgarh, Dhurmeti and Gogunda. Another known example is the fact that the Ujjainiya Rajputs of Bhojpur in the fourteenth century had to flee to the hills and forests after they were defeated by the Sharqi invaders of Jaunpur. Like Rana Pratap and countless other warrior clans in history, they employed the Vietcong-like strategy, and were, after a number of years or even decades, eventually able to reclaim their home ground.

Secondly, there is a curious yet undeniable connection of this clan with the gentle and long-living tortoise, an ancient land-dwelling reptile, several species (both tortoises and turtles) of which abound in the Chambal region. In this regard, it must be pointed out that the term 'Kachwaha' is, in fact, a fairly recent name adopted by this clan. During the time of Raja Man Singh I of Amber, the name the raja used for his own dynasty was 'Kurmba', which is the vernacularization of the Sanskrit *kurma*, literally translated to tortoise. While 'kaccha' refers to marsh or bog land. Kachapa could, thus, be translated as 'that which lives in the marsh', a term which brings to mind tortoises and other creatures dwelling in the winding river tributaries and the maze-like ravines of Gopaksetra.

Furthermore, tortoises of various species and sizes are, indeed, found in abundance in the Chambal region, coupled with the fact that the tortoise was a totem held sacred by this clan since ancient days. This is corroborated by A.H. Bingley, who was the foremost expert on the recruitment of Rajput sepoys during the late nineteenth and early twentieth centuries. According to his *Handbook on Rajputs*, he concurred that the name of this clan was derived from the Sanskrit *kachchapa*, which he translated as 'relating to tortoise', and speculated that the animal was a tribal god or totem.[52] There is, indeed, a shared belief among Kachwaha clansmen with regards to their reverence of the tortoise, which hints to the association with their ancestral land of Gopaksetra and the Chambal region.

Bearing these facts in mind, it seems logical that the Kachaphaghatas who ruled the area where the Kurmbas are said to have originated from, and who are also associated with the tortoise, are but one and the same family.

There is, however, an argument that the meaning of Kachaphaghata or Kacchapari is 'slayers of tortoise', which may indicate the possibility that the Kurmbas and Kachaphaghatas were enemies of one another, although there is no tradition/legend that suggests so. Bhatnagar, who conducted extensive research on this topic, has put this argument to rest with the reasoning that it is more likely that 'Kacchapa or Kurma is a shortened form of Kacchapaghata. If it is so, as seems likely, the possibility of Kacchapaghata and Kachwaha being of different stock, the former being slayers or enemies of the latter, as their designation implies, does not arise.' Bhatnagar further adds that 'this view is supported by inclusion of the Kacchapaghata princes of Gwalior in the genealogies given by Rajpana and Nansi.'[53]

One must bear in mind that the Kachaphaghatas were chiefly neighbours of the famed Chandelas of Khajuraho, the

[52]Bingley, A.H., *Handbook on Rajputs,* Asian Educational Services, New Delhi, 1986.

[53]Bhatnagar, V.S., *Life and Times of Sawai Jai Singh 1688–1743,* Impex India, Delhi, 1974, p. 4.

Paramaras of Malwa and the Chauhans of eastern Rajasthan. Each of these clans are known for their perseverance of the Vedic world view, the Sanskritic culture of their court, their subscription to traditional architectural treatises as well as their war-like demeanour, which indisputably reveals them to be inheritors of post-Gupta high culture of north India.

Numismatic evidence certainly seems to suggest so, as most-known Kachaphaghata coins were minted in a manner that had the name of the ruler in Devanagari script on one side and a stylized Lakshmi on the obverse. This style of coinage essentially originated from Gupta coinage, coupled with the fact that the weight of the coin was maintained at 3.6 grams (or four and a half *masha*).

With regards to the mutation of the clan's name, Bhatnagar's reasoning seems most logical—Kachaphaghatas would have, indeed, been an eloquent name for the rulers of Gopaksetra, as the high culture of post-Gupta north India eroded in the passing centuries and the increasingly chaotic geopolitical climate emerged in the region. The shortened name of Kachapa/Kurma/Kurmba would have been more practical epithet in an age of total war, while it still retained the essential reminder of the revered tortoise. Additionally, the Balvan inscription of the Chauhans of Ranthambore (dated 1288 CE) mentions conflict between Jaitrasimha, successor of Vagbhata of Ranthambore, and several rulers, including the 'Kurma ruler' of Amrapuri (Amber).[54] This inscription is an additional confirmation that

[54]Sharma, Dasharatha, *Early Chauhān Dynasties: A Study of Chauhān Political History, Chauhān Political Institution, and Life in the Chauhān Dominions, from 800 to 1316 A.D.*, Motilal Banarsidass Publishers, Delhi, 1975, p. 121.

following their move into Dhundhar during the time of Dulha Rai throughout the shift to Amber, the Kachaphaghatas came to be known as the Kurmas (Kurmbas). Additionally, it must be noted that the Kachaphaghatas were known patrons of Vaishnavism, Shaivism, Shaktism and Jainism. The name of Maharajadhiraja Vajradaman is found at the base of a Jain image dated VS 1034 (977–978 CE).[55] The Jain images of Gwalior Fort are also visible to all visitors. Jain rock-cut figures are also found on the fort rock at Gwalior, while Jain artefacts are found throughout the Kachaphaghatas domains of Sihonia, Padhavali, Narwar, Sesai, Bhimpur as well as Dubkund, among other places. The patronization of Jainism is a trait characteristic of this clan even with their migration into Dhundhar, through to the founding of Jainagara (Jaipur), which, till date, is a center of a large and prosperous Jain community.

Lastly, there is the often-ignored fact that in the earliest epigraphic records of the Kachwahas, they introduce the founder of their various branches as 'Kacchapaghata-Vamsatilaka' or 'Kacchapaghatanvaya-sarah-kamala-martanda'[56], conclusively solidifying the linkage between the Kurmas and the Kachaphaghatas. Therefore, the ancestral link between the Kachwahas of Dhundhar and the Kachaphaghatas of Gopaksetra should be seen as fact rather than myth.[57]

---

[55]Willis, Michael D., *Inscriptions of Gopaksetra: Materials for the History of Central India*, British Museum Press, 1996.

[56]Ray, H.C., *The Dynastic History of Northern India: Early Medieval Period*, Munshiram Manoharlal, New Delhi, 1973, p. 821.

[57]For further information on the mutation of the clan's name please see Appendix II.

Branches of the Kachaphaghata Family

According to Michael D. Willis and Ahmed Ali, there is a consensus that there were three branches of the Kachaphaghatas that were recorded rulers of Gopaksetra. As shall be explored in Chapter 3, their association with the area was much earlier than the mid-tenth century, which is simply when they re-established the sovereignty of Gwalior Raj in Gopaksetra. A list of the rulers from the three known branches of the Kachaphaghata dynasty is given below:

Gwalior Branch

Laksamana (950–975 CE)
Vajradaman (975–995 CE)
Mangalaraja (995–1015 CE)
Kirttiraja (1015–1035 CE)
Muladeva (Bhuvanapala or Devabratta) (1035–1055 CE)
Devapala (1055–1075 CE)
Padampala (1075–1080 CE)
Mahipala (1080–1104 CE)
Ratnapala
Madhusudana
Tejkarana

Dubkund Branch

Yuvraja (c. 1000 CE)
Arjuna (c. 1015–1035 CE)
Abhimanyu (1035–1044 CE)
Vijayapala (c. 1044–1070 CE)
Vikrama Simha (c. 1070–1100 CE)

Narwar Branch
Gagan Simha (c. 1075–1090 CE)
Sarad Simha (c. 1090–1105 CE)
Vira Simha (c. 1105–1125 CE)

The list of Kachchaphaghata rulers has been charted by Willis and Ahmed Ali in their valuable works, *Inscriptions of Gopaksetra* and *Kachchhapaghata Art and Architecture*. The Gwalior geological line is based on the Sas-Bahu Temple inscription of 1093 CE within Gwalior Fort, while the line of the Narwar branch is based on the Nalapur Mahadurg Grant of 1120 CE.[58]

Dasharatha Sharma, however, draws a slightly different chart of Kachaphagata rulers of Gwalior[59], as shown below:

Dholā
|
Laksmana
|
Vajradāmā (built the Gwalior Fort)
|
Mangalarāyā
|
Kritarāya
|
Mūladeva
|

[58]Hooja, Rima, *A History of Rajasthan*, Rupa & Co., New Delhi, 2006, p. 389.
[59]Sharma, Dasharatha, *Rajasthan Through the Ages*, Vol. 1, Rajasthan State Archives, Bikaner, 1966, pp. 693–94.

Padamapāla
|
Sūrapāla
|
Mahīpāla
|
18 generations more of rulers with their names ending in Pāla
|
Revakāhina
|
Īsāsimha
|
Sodhasimha
|
Dūlhadeva (gave Gwalior to his maternal nephew)
|
Hanumān
|
Kākaladeva (founder of Āmer)

Here, it must be noted that in local tradition, Vajradaman is not remembered for building the fortress of Gwalior; however, he is known from epigraphic records as having defeated the Pratiharas in battle and ousting them from Gwalior. Additionally, it must be pointed out the epithet of 'Pal', which translates to 'protector' in Prakrit, was in popular usage among the Kshatriyas of north India during the early medieval period.[60] This usage is comparable to how 'Singh' gained prominent usage among Rajputs for much of the past five centuries.

[60]Most notably but not exclusively with the Pala rulers of Bihar and Bengal, one of the three most powerful dynasties of India from the eighth to early twelfth centuries.

THREE

EARLY HISTORY OF THE KACHWAHAS

Kachaphaghatas and the Imperial Pratiharas

Now that we have a better view of the emergence of the Kachaphaghatas, let us briefly examine the context of their kingdom in the political climate of early medieval north India between the eighth and eleventh centuries. In order to do so, I have pieced together information from various sources, which alludes to relevant epigraphic records, Islamic records, such as the *Tabakat-i-Akbari* and the *Tarikh-i-Firishta*, as well as the interpretation of modern historians.

According to Michael D. Willis, in his valuable work *Inscriptions of Gopaksetra*, 'the Candellas, Paramaras and Kacchapaghatas shared a common origin as tributaries of the leading powers; when their overlords faltered in the mid-tenth century, they assumed increasing power and independence.'[61]

The leading power in this case was the Pratiharas, known alternately in an inscription as the Gurjara-Pratiharas, the dynasty that gave its name to Gujarat and dominated much of north-west India following the decline of Harshavardhana's famed but short-lived empire in the mid-seventh century. At the height of their power, this dynasty was known as the Imperial Pratiharas.

It is imperative to stress the fact that the geopolitical landscape of central India at that time was, like much of north India, dependent on the fortunes of Harshavardhana's imperial capital of Kanyakubja (Kannauj)[62], which now became the bone of contention among the great powers of north India.

The Tripartite Struggle between the Palas, Pratiharas and Rashtrakutas

The Kachaphaghatas, having established their rule in Gwalior, Narwar, Sihonia and Dubkund, continued to rule the area more or less throughout the rise and fall of Harshavardhana. It seems that due to the naturally guarded landscape of Gopeksetra, they were not directly affected by the eastwards March of the Pratiharas, who swept in from Rajasthan and captured all that lay between Mandavyapura (Mandore), the original and western capital of the Pratihara domain, and

---

[61]Willis, Michael D., *Inscriptions of Gopaksetra: Materials for the History of Central India,* British Museum Press, 1996.

[62]It was also known by the name Mahodaya in the Barah copper plate inscription of the Pratihara ruler Mihir Bhoja (Bhoja I).

the imperial city of Kannauj, situated to the north-west of Gopaksetra. This Pratihara expansion into central India began during the reign of the Pratihara ruler Vatsaraja (r. 777–79 CE), who earned the imperial greatness that his descendants would come to enjoy.

Kannauj was, at that time, ruled by a king known as Indrayudha, who is said to have been a descendent of Harshavardhana. His lineage gave him great prestige as the nominal lord of north India, although he has been compared to the later Mughals after Aurangzeb who were little more than figure heads, while the political and military powers lay in the hands of various warlords who were their supposed vassals.

The desire to be the overlord of Kannauj led Vatsaraja into conflict with the great Pala ruler Dharmapala, who shared the same ambition, and the two armies clashed in a great battle somewhere in the Gangetic Doab region, in which Vatsaraja is said to have emerged victorious. His days of glory were, however, short-lived, as he was defeated by the surprise northwards march of the Rashtrakuta king Dhruva Dharavarsha (r. 780–93 CE). The scenario at that time is aptly described by the great historian A.L. Basham:

> The Palas of eastern India were the first to gain the ascendancy, and for a while, in the early part of the 9th century were the masters of Kanyakubja. The long reign of the great king Dharmapala (c. 770 – 810) marks the apogee of the Pala power; by the time of his death control of Kanyakubja was lost, but his successor, Devapala (c. 810 – 850), was still a very important king,

> who was in diplomatic contact with the Sailendra kings of Sumatra...
>
> In the 9th century and 10th centuries, the Gurjara-Pratiharas, who probably originated in Rajasthan, were the masters of Kanyakubja, and the most powerful kings of northern India. They successfully resisted the Arabs, who in 712 had occupied Sind, and who for over a century made frequent attacks on their eastern neighbours. The two most powerful Pratihara kings, Mihira Bhoja (c. 840–885) and Mahendrapala (c. 885–910), pushed back the Palas, and were overlords of most of northern India as far as the borders of Bengal. But they were weakened by the repeated invasions of the Rastrakutas of the Deccan, who, in 916, temporarily occupied Kanyakubja. These persistent raids from the south seems to have turned the attention of the Pratihara kings away from the north-west, where now new forces were gathering which were ultimately to over throw Hindu India. Though the Pratiharas regained their capital after its occupation by the Rastrakutas, they never regained their strength, and throughout the 10th century the Pratiharas feudatories grew more and more powerful at the expense of their former masters.[63]

Vatsaraja then lost hold of all the gains in central India and had to retreat back to the safety of the Rajasthani dessert. Interestingly, Dhruva, brimming with confidence over his victory against the Pratiharas is also said to have marched to

[63]Basham, A.L., *The Wonder That was India*, Grove Press, New York, 1954, pp. 70–71.

battle Dharmapala. However, realistically, Dhruva's supplies must have been overstretched, while Dharmapala was near his home ground and would have been in a better position to field fresh forces, which led to Dhruva's march homewards without consolidating territory gains in north India but laden with riches and war booty nonetheless.

The next great challenge faced by the local powers of central India was the ascendency of the Palas, who took advantage of the Pratihara's defeat and the Rashtrakuta's unwillingness to hold on to these northern territories and occupied Kannauj. This must have been a proud moment for the great Pala emperor Dharmapala, who is believed to have held a grand durbar there and then proceeded to replace Vatsaraja's nominee to the throne of Kannauj, Indrayudha, with his own candidate Chakrayudha[64], who is believed to have been from the same lineage. This was again followed by an imperial durbar in which Dharmapala recieved the submission of of numerous vassal rulers. Therefore, the installation of Chakrayudha was an act that not only pronounced the apogee of Pala power in north India but was also said to have been an acclaimed move by the local rulers, who were apparently more threatened by the ambition and methods of Vatsaraja.

Nonetheless, after Dharmapala was succeeded by his son Devapala (r. 810–50 CE), the Pratiharas returned with astounding force, this time led by Vatsaraja's successor Nagabhatta II (r. 805–33 CE), who was able to march back

[64]The conflict between Dharmapala continued with Govind III (r. 793–814 CE), the successor of Dhruva Dharavarsha.

from Rajasthan into central India, as is noted by historian Rima Hooja, 'Vanguishing the lord of Vanga (Bengal), Nagabhata II seized the hill-forts of the kings of Anarta, Malava, Matsya, Kirata, Turushka and Vatsa.'[65]

Nagabhatta II also defeated Chakrayudha, who was installed on the throne of Kannauj by the Palas. The Gwalior Prashasti inscription of his grandson, Bhoja I, proudly proclaims his victories and it must have been clear to all the rulers of north India that the fortune and power of the Pratiharas was now on the rise and unstoppable for the time being.[66] In fact, the Pratihara Empire was now on par with the Guptas in terms of territorial size and longevity, or at the very least, it was longer lasting and more stable than Harshavardhana's short-lived empire, whose last descendant, Chakrayudha, was ousted by the Pratiharas. The descendants of Nagabhata II were to hold on to Imperial Kannauj for the next 200 years. Their most powerful rulers of this period being Mihira Bhoja (r. 840–85 CE) and Mahendrapala (r. 885–910 CE).

The Loss and Reclamation of Gwalior and the Rise of the Chandelas

Gopaksetra being a provincial power, it must have been clear to the Kachaphaghata leaders that it was a wiser policy to preserve their domain and become feudatories of the behemoths—the Palas and then the Pratiharas (from the

[65]Hooja, Rima, *A History of Rajasthan*, Rupa & Co., New Delhi, 2006, p. 185.
[66]Ibid.

time of Nagabhata II). They were certainly not alone in their persuasion of this policy, which seems to have been adopted by other clans such as the Chandelas and the Paramaras, among others. The Chauhans of Shakambari and the Guhilas were also known feudatories who fought for the Imperial Pratiharas during this time. Whether or not or in what manner the Kachaphaghatas had to react to the occasional incursion of the Rashtrakutas into north India is an issue we could only speculate upon. On the other hand, contacts with the northern-based Pratiharas and Palas must have been more consistent, given the geographical and cultural affinity of the northerners.

It was most likely during the time of Nagabhatta II, in the ninth century, that the fortress of Gwalior was once again snatched away from the Kachaphaghatas and went into Pratihara possession. This is evident from the Gwalior Prashasti inscription of Bhoja I,[67] who is often regarded by historians as the greatest of the Imperial Pratiharas (and is famous for his unusual Adivaraha or boar-incarnation of lord Vishnu coin). We also know that, based on an inscription dated 876 CE, following the annexation of Gwalior by the Pratiharas, a hereditary Brahmin known as Alla was appointed by the imperial lords of Kannauj to be *kottapala* or warden of the fortress.[68] Gwalior was, after all, an important fortress that protected the southern flank of the imperial capital of Kannauj. Keeping in mind the periodic invasions

---

[67]Ibid.

[68]Majumdar, R.C. (ed.), *The Age of Imperial Kanauj*, Bharatiya Vidya Bhavan, Bombay, 1955, p. 240.

by the Rashtrakutas, who marched northwards following river routes, it is no surprise that the Imperial Pratiharas would deem it necessary to directly control such a strategic fortress.

While the fact that the Pratiharas held Gwalior between the ninth and tenth centuries is not disputed, of equal relevance is the need to acknowledge that the rest of the region was still in the hands of the local chieftains, who were, for the time being, bound under Pratihara suzerainty. It must also be emphasized here that the legend pertaining to the founding of Gwalior Fort is associated with the Kachaphaghatas and not the Pratiharas or other Rajput clans.

The paramount power of the Pratiharas in north and central India during this period was, however, not without challenges, a major factor being the continuous tripartite struggle against both the Rastrakutas of the Deccan, and the Palas of Bihar/Bengal, which caused a huge drain in terms of men and material to all sides. Another consequence of the tripartite struggle was the instability and constantly shifting political boundaries, which, nonetheless, gave an opportunity for the regional powers to consolidate their hold and take advantage of the prevailing climate to suit their enterprise. One such clan that was able to take advantage of the prevailing situation was the Chandelas (from the Sanskrit *Candratreya*), who are said to have been an indigenous family that, by the early tenth century, firmly rose to power in the area known as Jejakabhukti[69] (to the immediate west of Gopaksetra). By the time of the Mughal period, this area

[69]Mitra, Sisir Kumar, *The Early Rulers of Khajuraho*, Motilal Banarsidass, Delhi, 1977, p. 29–20.

became known as Bundhelkhand. The Chandela's rise is said to have been acknowledged by the Imperial Pratiharas, who recognized them as a vassal chieftain. However, the Khajuraho (Khajraho) inscription records that the Chandela ruler Harsha (r. 900–25 CE) came to the aid of the Pratihara king Kshitipaladeva (identified as Mahipala I) and reinstate him on the throne of Kannauj. This is interpreted by historians as Harsha having assisted Mahipala I to recover Kannauj after it was lost to the Rashtrakuta ruler Indra III in about 914 CE.[70] This successful act initiated the meteoric rise in prestige and political influence of the Chandelas within the ailing Pratihara Empire, and they have been equated as the viceroys of these later Pratihara rulers of Kannauj.

Towards the mid-tenth century, after the death of the Pratihara emperor Mahipala I, the Imperial Pratihara domain began its long terminal decline throughout north India. An internal conflict of succession seems to have plagued them, demonstrated by the fact that after the demise of Mahipala I, although he was succeeded by his son Vinayakpala (ruled until 942 CE), we next hear of at least four Pratihara rulers within a span of 15 years.[71] During the time of Vinayakpala, the grim outlook for the Pratihara Empire became a reality, as sometime between 937 and 940 CE, they had to face a massive invasion led by Rashtrakuta forces under Krishna III.

---

[70]Majumdar, R.C. (ed.), *The Age of Imperial Kanauj*, Bharatiya Vidya Bhavan, Bombay, 1955, p. 84.

[71]Vinayakapala ruled until about 942 CE, and was succeeded by Mahendrapala II (945–46 CE). He was followed by Devapala (948–49 CE), Vinayakapala II (953–54) Mahipala II (955 CE) and Vijaypala (960 CE); Majumdar, R.C. (ed.), *The Age of Imperial Kanauj*, Bharatiya Vidya Bhavan, Bombay, 1955, p. 135.

The Rashtrakuta records attest the fact that the important citadels of Chitrakuta (Chittor) and Kalanjara (Kalinjar) were snatched away from the Pratiharas.[72] The main force of the Deccan power, however, seems to have disbanded and eventually marched proudly southwards having gained major victory and one would imagine large quantities of loot at the expense of the Pratiharas of Kannauj.

The loss of resources from the continuous tripartite conflict coupled with this internal succession dispute seems to provide an explanation for the rapid decline and disintegration of Imperial Pratihara power, which led the various mahasamantas or feudatories in Rajasthan as well as in central India gradually asserting their independence. In central India, in particular, the strongest among the mahasamantas, namely the Chandelas and the Kachaphaghatas, also saw the chance to break free from Pratihara overlordship.

The Chandela ruler Yasovarman, son and successor to Harsha, was a very successful military leader in his own right. Initially, like his father, he seems to have nominally recognized Pratihara suzerainty and his role as the powerful agent of the Pratiharas of Kannauj. However, his desire for power is revealed from the fact that he was able to convince and obtain from the Pratihara emperor Devapala a golden murti of Vaikuntha Vishnu[73], which is said to have originated from the sacred Mount Kailash. The Imperial Pratiharas

[72]Majumdar, R.C. (ed.), *The Age of Imperial Kanauj*, Bharatiya Vidya Bhavan, Bombay, 1955, p. 14.

[73]Goetz, Hermann, 'The Historical Background of the Great Temples of Khajuraho', *Arts Asiatiques*, vol. 5, no. 1 (1958), pp. 35–47.

are said to have received this idol from the Shahi rulers of Kabul, who in turn claims to have have received it from the lord of the Bhotas (Tibetans). Now, in many Asian nations, the transfer of a stately murti from one city to another is often equated with the transfer of power, and, indeed, this event is recorded as being the most celebrated occasion in the Chandelas' chronicles.[74] It was also the chief reason that Lakshmana[75] temple at Khajuraho was commissioned by Yasovarman Chandela.

Confident of his rising power, Yasovarman also took advantage of the Pratiharas' inability to retake control of their domain[76] and further seized the famed fortress of Kalinjar for himself. It has been suggested that the reconquest of the region by Yasovarman's successor Dhanga, following the Rashtrakutas invasion sometime in the 940s, coupled with the inability of the Pratiharas to reoccupy their fortress inadvertently turned Dhanga into the first independent Chandela ruler.

Having captured Kalinjar and consolidating his hold, Yasovarman proved his military might by successfully attacking his southern neighbours—the Kalachuris of Chedi as well as the Paramaras (Parmars) of Malwa, who were mahasamantas of the Rashtrakuta emperor Krishna III. This aggressive policy against both of his southern neighbours was perhaps a response to the Rashtrakuta invasion of the north about a decade earlier, in which the Kalachuris and Paramara

---

[74]Majumdar, R.C. (ed.), *The Age of Imperial Kanauj*, Bharatiya Vidya Bhavan, Bombay, 1955.

[75]The temple was then consecrated by Yasovarman's successor, Dhanga, in 954 CE.

[76]From the Kathiawar peninsula to the Gangetic Doab.

contingents must have taken part. Nonetheless, this act was to have serious consequences by the time of his descendent Vijaypala Chandela (r. 1035–50 CE) and seems to bear relation to the cause of the Kachaphaghata scion Dulha Rai's death, as recorded in the *Kachawan Ri Vanshavali*, which states that he 'left for Gwalior on a request from there, to fight with the enemy who had come from the Deccan'; the date of this event given in the text is VS 1093 (1036 CE).[77]

Keeping in mind this scenario of political relations in central India in the late tenth century, the event which transpires next is of great significance to the subject concerned—the retaking of Gwalior by the Kachaphaghata ruler Vajradaman (r. 975–95 CE). Having bided their time for over a century, Vajradaman must have been confident in his recognition of the breakdown of Pratihara suzerainty, as he seized the opportunity to attack Gwalior and reclaim his ancestral possession.

It was possibly out of Narwar[78] that Vajradaman's forces marched northwards to successfully reclaim the prized ancestral citadel of Gwalior. If this were the case, it would have given the Kachaphaghatas the advantage of fighting within familiar terrain, a short marching distance from their home ground.

It is clear that Vajradaman's objective of reclaiming Gwalior was by all means achieved as recorded in the earliest

[77]Ratnawat, Shyam Singh (ed.), *Kachhawan Ri Vanshavali: A Genealogical Account of the Kacchawa Nobility*, Centre for Rajasthan Studies, University of Jaipur, Jaipur, 1981.

[78]Although it was located within the disintegrating Pratihara Empire, Narwar and the surrounding settlements of Gopaksetra were still the domain of the Kachaphaghatas.

surviving epigraphic reference to the Kachaphaghatas. The notable Sas-Bahu temple inscription ascribes the deed of the Kachaphaghata rulers Laksamana (r. 950–75 CE) and his successor Vajradaman.[79] According to the inscription, Maharajadhiraja Vajradaman, the successor of Laksamana, 'put down the rising power of the ruler of Gandhinagara (Kannauj) and his proclamation drum resounded on the fort of Gopadri.'

This record points to the fact that the Kachaphaghatas gained victory over the Pratiharas (of Kannauj) and captured (recaptured) the fort of Gwalior (which their august ancestor Suraj Pal is said to have founded). This is the most important surviving record of the Gwalior branch of the Kachaphaghatas, according to the noted historian V.S. Bhatnagar.[80] Based on the interpretation of Pratihara records, such as the Rakhetra stone inscription of Vinayakpala dated VS 999–1000, Sisir Kumar Mitra states that the Gurjara-Pratiharas must have lost the fortress of Gwalior to the Kachaphaghatas sometime between 944–977 CE, which as mentioned is confirmed by the Sas-Bahu inscription. Additionally, contemporary evidence indicates that there was widespread internal dissensions in the Pratihara domain, which, coupled with fresh Rashtrakuta attacks by Krishna III in about 963 CE, facilitated the conditions for the Kachaphaghatas to march out and successfully reconquer Gwalior.[81]

---

[79]Willis, Michael D., *Temples of Gopaksetra: A Regional History of Architecture and Sculpture in Central India AD 600–900,* British Museum Press, 1997, p. 26.
[80]Bhatnagar, V.S., *Life and Times of Sawai Jai Singh 1688–1743*, Impex India, Delhi, 1974.
[81]Mitra, Sisir Kumar, *The Early Rulers of Khajuraho*, Motilal Banarsidass, Delhi,

The eminent historian H.C. Ray concurs to this view and states that the Kachaphaghatas were initially feudatories of the Imperial Pratiharas until they conquered the fortress of Gwalior by defeating the forces of the ruler of Kannauj, who he identified as the Pratihara ruler Vijayapala.[82]

This event also seems to have initiated an alliance, or at the very least the possibility of cooperation between Dhangadeva Chandela and the Kachaphaghatas under the leadership of Vajradaman. For reasons unbeknown to us[83], Dhangadeva, upon seeing Vajradaman's successful retaking of Gwalior, decided to align himself with the Kachaphaghatas (who were his immediate neighbours to the west) rather than the ailing Pratiharas of Kannauj. Although the exact details of the agreement between Vajradaman and Dhangadeva has not come down to us, Islamic sources chronicling the career of Mahmud of Ghazni does point out to an alliance between the Chandelas and the Kachaphaghatas.[84] This is coupled with the fact that the Chandelas and Kachaphaghatas subsequently joined forces in fighting against their various common enemies, as shall be demonstrated in the following section.

Additionally, Mitra notes that the Khajuraho inscription of VS 1011, described the area of the Chandela kingdom as

---

1977, p. 58.

[82]Ray, H.C., *The Dynastic History of Northern India: Early Medieval Period*, Munshiram Manoharlal, New Delhi, 1973.

[83]Perhaps it was some shared religious belief or ideology that led to the political alliance.

[84]Muhammad Nazim, *The Life and Times of Sultan Mahmud of Ghazna*, Cambridge University Press, 2014.

bordering 'the mountain of Gopa' (Gwalior). According to Mitra, 'It must be concluded that the Candella episode, and the Kacchapaghata episode connected with the conquest of Gopadri are not separate stories, but that they refer to a single event in which the Candellas and the Kachaphaghatas were closely associated together.'[85]

After this episode of regaining of Gwalior Fort, the conflict between the Pratiharas of Kannauj and the alliance of the Chandelas and the Kachaphaghatas continued on from the tenth to the eleventh centuries. Some historians commenting on this alliance attempt to depict the Kachaphaghatas as being a feudatory of the Chandelas; however, this is mere speculation, as there is no clear evidence to suggest so. But the fact that they were allies could be irrefutably proven.

It must be noted that the Chandelas and Kachaphaghatas were by no means the only factions that were taking advantage of the disintegration of Pratihara power and its overstretched domain. After all, despite all the setback suffered, the Pratihara Empire still stretched from Saurashtra (the Kathiawar peninsula) through much of Rajasthan and across Malwa into central India. Other clans that became powerful in the following centuries also took advantage of the Imperial Pratihara's disintegration, examples being the usurping of Chitrakuta led by Bhartrapatta II, the Guhila chief or Mularaj Chalukya's usurpation of the Pratiharas' former domain in Gujarat and setting up of his capital at

[85]Mitra, Sirir Kumar, *The Early Rulers of Khajuraho*, Motilal Banarsidass, Delhi, 1977, p. 59.

Anhillapattan.[86] Then there is the fact that the Chauhan chiefs of Nadol as well as Shakambari also rose up against their imperial overlords.

One could rightly argue that following the mid-ninth century, as the power and prestige of the Chandelas, Paramaras, Guhilas, Chauhans and Kachaphaghatas rose, that of the Imperial Pratiharas declined. The Pratiharas were eventually left to rule the great metropolis of Kannauj and its surrounding pockets, although the air of past glory was still associated with them for the time being.

The Ghaznavid Invasion of North India, the Demise of the Shahis and Pratiharas, and Role of the Chandelas and Kachaphaghatas

The Ghaznavid Sultanate arose from the ashes of Persia's first Islamic state, the Samaniyan or Samanid Empire. Alptigin was the commander-in-chief of the Samanid army, but having forsaken the rulers of Bukhara, he set up his own base of power in eastern Afghanistan, with his headquarters at Ghazni. In 975 CE, he was succeeded by his slave-commander Sabuktigin, who, through his sheer will, consolidated his domain to become a ruler in his own right. Sabuktigin began the Ghaznavid expansionist policy and was, in 997 CE, succeeded by his son the renowned Mahmud of Ghazni (r. 997–1030 CE). Despite the pompous claims and praiseworthy language employed by the Persian chroniclers, most historians concur that Mahmud's infamous excursions

[86] Hooja, Rima, *A History of Rajasthan*, Rupa & Co., 2006, New Delhi, p. 190.

into India were more to do with plundering India's legendary wealth as opposed to territorial conquests.[87]

Additionally, with regards to the topic at hand, the Islamic chronicles greatly help to fill in the gap in terms of events that transpired but came to be lost or unrecorded by the various Hindu factions.

Towards the end of the tenth century, the Hindu kingdom which bore the brunt of the famed Turkic and central-Asian horse-archer contingents under the command of Amir Sabuktigin was the Shahi kingdom based in the Hindu Kush region and eastern Punjab, ruled by Jayapala. The defeat of Jayapala's army in 977 CE resulted in the territory west of the Indus, including Peshwar and Lamghan, being annexed by the Ghaznivids, although, for the time being, it still had no direct impact on other states of north India.

Talking about Mahmud of Ghazni's later forays into India, Mitra records:

> Then again in 1006-07 AD, when Sultan Mahmud in course of his invasion of Multan tried to pass through the territories of Anandapala, the successor of Jayapala, the latter apprehending a crisis for the whole of India, appealed to the neighbouring Rajas for help. The Rajas of Ujjain, Gwalior, Kalinjar, Kannauj, Delhi and Ajmer, according to Firishta, readily responded to the appeal and despatched their contingents to swell the Sahi army.[88]

[87]His objective of territorial conquest lay towards Iran and fending off central Asian Turkic hordes; however, these objectives were to be funded by the amazing wealth captured from the hit-and-run raids into north India.

[88]Mitra, Sisir Kumar, *The Early Rulers of Khajuraho*, Motilal Banarsidass, Delhi, 1977.

Gwalior, at that time, as we know, was under the rule of the Kachaphaghatas. The outcome of the battle was, however, in the favour of the Ghaznavid invaders, who pursued the defenders up to the fort of Nagarkot.[89]

It is noted by Mitra that despite the loss inflicted on Anandapala and his allied forces, the main territory of those allies (in north India and central India) were yet to be directly affected. However, the scenario was to change in the course of 10 years, as with the conquest of the Shahi kingdom completed, it was now the turn of the weakened Prathihras, who in their bygone days of glory had led the vanguard against the early Islamic incursions into India, to bear the brunt of determined efforts of Mahmud of Ghazni. According to Mitra:

> The black cloud of the Gaznavid invasions looming large on the north-western horizon of India since the time of Dhanga (famed ruler of the Chandellas), gradually assumed greater and more menacing proportions. The victory of Sultan Mahmud against the Sahi (Shahi) rulers in 1008 AD, opened up the road to India beyond the Sutlej to the Turki depredations, which from now on were almost regularly carried out year after year till they appeared in Kanauj in 409 AH ie, 1018 AD.[90]

The Pratiharas were, at that time, under the leadership of Rajyapala, who still ruled the imperial city of Kannauj. However, his sovereignty over his feudatories was all but illusionary, and

[89]Ibid. 68.

[90]Ibid. 72.

as a matter of fact, due to reasons unbeknown to us, he was abandoned, it seems, by almost all of them, as no major raja is recorded to have come to his aid. Rajyapala, with no army to command except for the garrison of Kannauj, retreated to the safety of a place called Bari, while Mahmud of Ghazni encountered no resistance as he captured and plundered Kannauj.[91] This being the main objective of this particular expedition, Mahmud returned to Ghazni, his caravans and elephants loaded with unimaginable wealth and loot.

Following the sack of Kannauj by Sultan Mahmud, Rajyapala had to face the ridicule and insults from his former allies, led by Vidyadhara (the Chandela ruler, who is recorded in Islamic chronicles as Bida, equivalent to vidya). The situation is described thus in a record of Sultan Mahmud's life: 'Shortly after the departure of sultan Mahmud in Sha 'ban 409, Ganda the Chandel Raja of Kalinjar, reproached Rajyapal of Kanauj for his pusillanimous flight from Sultan Mahmud and formed a league against him with the neighbouring rajas including Arjan, Raja of Gwalior.'[92]

According to Mitra, Vidyadhara[93] had an irreconcilable quarrel with Rajyapala, apparently due to the latter's flight

[91]This is not dissimilar to the manner in which the later Mughal emperors (after Aurangzeb), despite their majestic heritage, were in several instances abandoned by their supposed protectors, and were left to face the depredations of various hostile forces, who were more than happy to carry away the accumulated wealth of Mughal cities.

[92]Muhammad Nazim, *The Life and Times of Sultan Mahmud of Ghazna*, Cambridge University Press, 2014, p. 110.

[93]Recorded in the Islamic sources as Ganda, who was actually Vidyadhara's father.

and surrender of his territories to the Mussalmans.[94] It must be noted, Chandelas were, until a few decades earlier, content in their role as a premier power within the Pratihara domain. But by 1019, however, their policy had reversed to the extent that they refused to fight on behalf of the rulers of Kannauj. We next know, based on the Dubkund inscription of the Kachaphaghata, that Arjuna Kachchapaghata is said to have killed Rajyapala Pratihara in a great battle.[95] As the Chandela–Kachchaphaghata alliance was still in existence during this period, Mitra observes that Arjuna must have been fighting on the instigation of the Chandelas.[96]

It may be observed that both Indian and Islamic sources clearly point that there was an acute conflict between Rajyapala of Kannauj and a coalition of rulers led by Vidyadhara, the Chandela king, and the Kachaphaghatas under Kirttiraja (of Gwalior) as well as Arjuna Kachaphaghata of the Dubkund branch. This was the culmination of the long-standing conflict between the remnants of the Imperial Pratiharas and the coalition of the Chandelas and the Kachaphaghatas. While the ruler of Gwalior at the time is recorded to be Kirttiraja, the ruler who is credited with the slaying of the Pratihara monarch is recorded as Arjuna. According to both Indian and Islamic sources, this victory is said to have considerably increased the prestige of the Chandela ruler Vidyadhara, who followed the

[94]Mitra, Sisir Kumar, *The Early Rulers of Khajuraho*, Motilal Banarasidass, Delhi, 1977.

[95]Willis, Michael D., *Inscriptions of Gopaksetra: Materials for the History of Central India*, British Museum Press, 1996, p. 6.

[96]Mitra, Sisir Kumar, *The Early Rulers of Khajuraho*, Motilal Banarasidass, Delhi, 1977.

footsteps of his predecessor in reducing Pratihara dominance and was now seen to be the first among the kings of north India. Vidyadhara then proceeded to install Trilochanapala as his 'puppet emperor' of Kannauj and successor to the slain Rajyapala. This setup, however, did not last long due to the interference of external forces, being the Ghaznavid threat. Thus, we find the Vidyadhara, who came to be regarded as the most powerful ruler of (north) India, devoted himself mainly to the task of resisting the encroachments of Islam and he is credited with the capture of the last remnants of the Pratihara power, which practically saddled him on to imperial status.[97]

We also know that not long after the defeat of Rajyapala, there was evidently a resumption of the traditional hostility between the Parmaras of Malwa and the Chandelas, which seemed to have briefly paused during the first Ghaznavid raid into central India. This is confirmed by the fact that there is a record of an attack by the Paramara ruler Bhoja, which was thwarted by the Kachaphaghata ruler Kirttiraja. According to Mitra:

> But in the Sas Bahu record, we are told that the Kacchapaghata prince Kirtiraja defeated the countless host of the prince of Malwa. The Malwa army received such a terrible shock on the occasion that the spears fell from their hands through fear, and were subsequently collected by the villagers (apparently of Gwalior) and heaped around their houses. The 'Malava-bhumipa' has generally been identified with the Paramara King

[97]Ibid. 83.

Bhoja, who was by no means a less important ruler.[98]

Thus, one could garner from the Sas-Bahu and the Dubkund inscriptions that the Chandela–Kachaphaghata alliance gained much strength and prestige among the leading powers of north India. The alliance not only withstood but also deflected indigenous as well as foreign invasions, as shall be demonstrated. This Kachaphaghata victory over the Paramara army is believed to have occurred sometime between 1018 CE but before the year 1022 CE. K.C. Jain also concurs that the Paramara ruler of Malwa, Bhoja, attempted to capture Gwalior but was defeated by the Kachaphaghata ruler Kirttiraj.[99]

In 1019, Mahmud of Ghazni returned to north India intent on destroying Trilochanapala of Kannauj. According to Muhammad Nazim, author of *The Life and Times of Sultan Mahmud of Ghazna,* following the slaying of Rajyapala and installation of Trilochanapala, Vidyadhara is said to have promised another Trilochanapala, who was the son of the slain Shahi ruler Anandapala, to retrieve his ancestral kingdom from the Ghaznavid occupation. Once this news reached the ears of Mahmud of Ghazni, he marched out of Ghazni at the beginning of Autumn 410 (October 1019) in order to crush both Trilochanapalas (one being the last Pratihara ruler of Kannauj as well as his main supporter Vidyadhara. There is a confusion of the Islamic chroniclers between the Chandela

[98]Ibid.

[99]The proud claim to the success made by Vidyadhara might have been related to this incident.

Jain, K.C., *Malwa Through the Ages,* Motilal Banarsidass, Delhi, 1972, p. 348.

rulers, Ganda or Gandadeva, and his son Bida or Vidyadhara, as the events transpired during the time of Vidyadhara and not Gandadeva). The confusion is further complicated by the fact that there are two Trilochanapalas—one is the successor of Anandapala of the Hindu Shahi dynasty, and the other is the successor of the ill-fated Pratihara ruler Rajyapala of Kannauj. In this campaign, Mahmud's forces is said to have crossed the Ganges River at a locale below Hardwar.[100] The aim of this campaign was perhaps to prevent the reorganizing and strengthening of the Hindu rajas who now formed a broader alliance under the leadership of Vidyadhara.

Having defeated Trilochanapala of Kannauj and leveled the town of Bari, Mahmud of Ghazni next focused his war machine on the defeat of the Chandela ruler Vidyadhara and his vast host of allies, which would turn out to be a larger assemblage of forces seen even by the experienced eye of Mahmud of Ghazni. According to Muhammad Nazim, based on his translation of the Persian chronicles, the sultan was then faced by the advancement of the allied forces, which is recorded to have swelled up greatly to 1,45,000 foot soldiers, 36,000 cavalry and 640 elephants. While the accuracy of the number of troops as well as tribute/loot recorded in the various Islamic chronicles have often been questioned, one could garner the point the chronicler is trying to convey—that it was a large army that Mahmud encountered. Mahmud is said to have marshalled his smaller force while sending forth an ambassador to Vidyadhara,

[100]Muhammad Nazim, *The Life and Times of Sultan Mahmud of Ghazna*, Cambridge University Press, 2014, p. 111.

calling upon him to accept Islam and pay tribute in order that armed confrontation be avoided. However, Vidyadhara is said to have indignantly rejected this, instead preparing for battle.[101]

As pointed out earlier, Vidyadhara with his capital at Kalinjar was now seen to be the strongest ruler of north India with formidable power. The closest ally of Vidyadhara among the host of rajas who joined the warband were the Kachaphaghatas, both of the Gwalior and Dubkand (and possibly the Narwar) branches, who were undoubtedly a part of this vast host of contingents assembled, the scale of which finds mention in Nazim's translation:

> The Sultan now ascended an eminence to reconnoittre the position of the enemy, and his eyes met with a spectacle which for once shook his courage. He saw before him, as far as eyes could reach, an imposing panorama of camps, pavilions and embankments and he regretted having ventured so far. In his distress, he prostrated himself in prayer to seek divine assistance, which restored his drooping spirits, and in the evening a successful engagement of Abu Abdu'llah Muhammad at-Ta'I, commander of the advance guard, with a detachment of Ganda, dispelled the remaining gloom.[102]

Instead of being an epic battle of the early medieval period, what happened next could perhaps be described as an

[101]Ibid. 111–12.

[102]Ibid.

'anticlimax'. Mitra notes that according to the *Tarikh-al-Kamil* written by Ibn Al-Athir:

> Before effecting a direct clash the men of the sultan diverted the course of the river. Only then was it possible for Yaminuddaulah to send a party of his infantry to fight him (Bida), and the latter also sent out against him a similar number, and both the armies continued reinforcing their soldiers till the two opposing forces increased in numbers, and the battle became vehement. At last the night overtook them and parted them.[103]

Mitra argues that due to the diversion of the river during the night, the strategic value of the location chosen by Vidyadhara was lost, and rather than allowing Mahmud to force a battle in the morning, the Chandela ruler opted for a strategic withdrawal.[104] Thus, there was no battle, and the Islamic chronicles (which were essentially public-relation records for future generations, as are Hindu bardic lores) described it as a win for Mahmud.

> The following morning Sultan Mahmud dispatched his ambassador to Ganda, but he returned to report that the enemy's camp was deserted. Ganda, unaccountably stricken with panic, had fled from the field under cover of night. The sacrifice of Rajyapal had evidently not improved the morale of his chief persecutor.
>
> The sultan thanked god for this unexpected good

[103]Mitra, Sisir Kumar, *The Early Rulers of Khajuraho*, Motilal Banarsidass, Delhi, 1977.
[104]Ibid.

> luck and, after making sure that no ambush had been laid, he gave orders for the plundering of the camp of the enemy who had left behind all their valuables.[105]

With this unexpected triumph from what might have been a glaring defeat against a larger army on their home ground[106], Sultan Mahmud practically decided not to press his luck and marched back to Ghazni. The events from this campaign, however, seems to have deeply disturbed the sultan's mind, as after three years of rest, recuperation and fielding his men, the Ghaznavid army would march out again in 1022 CE (413 AH) with the specific intention of breaking the power of Vidyadhara and his allies. Among the closest allies of the Chandelas were the Kachaphaghatas, and, this time, it was their turn to face the wrath of Mahmud of Ghazni.

Siege of Gwalior by Mahmud

Mahmud of Ghazni, having been well rested for nearly three years, was intent on rectifying his inability to defeat Vidyadhara during the campaign of 1019–20 CE. From Ghazni, Mahmud marched directly to the domain of Vidyadhara. In the words of Nazim:

> The power of Ganda had not been broken in the expedition against him in 410 (1019–20) and he still openly defied the Sultan. In 413 (1022), therefore, the

[105]Muhammad Nazim, *The Life and Times of Sultan Mahmud of Ghazna*, Cambridge University Press, 2014, p. 112.

[106]There was no fight between the main forces of both the Hindu and Islamic armies, only clashes by the forward auxiliaries.

> Sultan again marched to Kalinjar to reduce him into submission. On his way thither the sultan passed the fort of Gwalior, The Raja of which, named Arjan, was a feudatory of Ganda. This fort was built on the summit of a stupendous rock and was reputed to be impregnable. The sultan stormed the fort, but failed to capture it. The raja despite successful resistance, was so alarmed that after four days he sued for peace, and made a present of 35 elephants.[107]

The above passage is a rather tame account among the usually boastful chronicles of Mahmud of Ghazni, in which he is often depicted as successfully storming forts, examples being his attacks on the Afshin Fort, Gharshistan, the fortress of Taq in Sistan, the fortress of Nargarkot, the fort of Munj (near modern Etawa), the forts of Asai, Sharwa (Sarawa near Meerut), Lodurva, among countless others. In Mahmud's chronicles, one regularly comes across him taking huge amounts of loot worth crores of dirhams and dinars (coins), capturing elephants in their hundreds (120, 350 elephants, etc.). However, in the case of the siege of Gwalior, which was the first mission on this particular expedition, it must be noted the peace offer was accepted with just 35 elephants and that too after just four days of fighting. We should now remember the fact that the fortress of Gwalior had, only a few years earlier, successfully thwarted the invasion and siege by the Paramara ruler Bhoja. After the victory over the Paramara army, the fort of Gwalior would have by all means been

[107]Muhammad Nazim, *The Life and Times of Sultan Mahmud of Ghazna*, Cambridge University Press, 2014, p. 113.

repaired, restocked and resupplied by the Kachaphaghata rulers to withstand any further invasion, and it seems that they were, thus, ably equipped to endure a prolonged siege.[108]

Mahmud of Ghazni must have realized that unlike the forts he encountered in other campaigns, the capture of Gwalior would require an impractically prolonged siege, in which case, his army could be outflanked by Vidyadhara's main forces, a situation somewhat comparable to that which Julius Caesar faced (but triumphed) in his iconic siege of Alesia in Gaul. Thus, Mahmud likely thought it more prudent to agree to a peace treaty with the Kachaphaghatas and move on to accomplish his primary objective, which was the defeat of Vidyadhara.

It is interesting to note that the ruler of the fort is recorded by Islamic sources as Arjuna Kachaphaghata rather than Kirttiraja. This may be due to confusion of the chroniclers, as they were already familiar with Arjuna from the episode pertaining to the slaying of Rajyapala, or due to other unknown reasons. There is a curious account recorded in Syriac with regards the settlement of the terms of peace after Mahmud's unsuccessful siege of Gwalior. In this record, a learned Arab was sent inside the castle as an ambassador, in which he spoke to the ruler of Gwalior through an interpreter. A condition of the peace treaty set out by Mahmud was that the Indian king must 'put on our clothes, tie a sword and belt round his waist and to ratify the oath, cut off the tip of

[108]These events occurred five centuries before artillery would be widely used in India. Akbar was able to conquer the illustrious fortresses of Chittor and Ranthambore with great difficulty, and that in an age when artillery was heavily employed.

his finger as is the Indian custom'. [109]

Apparently during the early medieval period, there was a custom among the Hindu rulers in north India that as a means of securing a treaty, it was customary to cut off the tip of the little finger of the rulers. It is interesting to note that the Arab ambassador was impressed with the youth and beauty of the Kachaphaghata king who sat on a silver throne, wearing a cloak, trousers and a turban. Additionally, the ambassador urged the king to put on the foreign clothes as per the agreement, but the Indian king only partially put on the belt 'and girded on the sword'. Lastly, after the ceremony, Mahmud is recorded to have sent to the raja 'a robe of honour, a turban, a belt, a gold caparisoned horse and a ring with his [Mahmud's] name inscribed on it'.[110]

Having secured a surprisingly modest peace treaty with the Kachaphaghata ruler, Mahmud then proceeded towards Kalinjar, eager to defeat Vidyadhara. Here again, Mahmud was faced with another impregnable citadel, and eventually another peace treaty was made. Mitra elaborates:

> Evidently like the Gwalior fort, the Kalanjar also could not be stormed by Mahmud in spite of his all-out efforts. It may be remembered that Mahmud set out on this expedition with a specific object of punishing Vidyadhara, but as an evident from the statements of Muslim historians, this was hardly achieved. Both the strongholds of Gwalior and Kalanjar remained unconquered and on

[109]Muhammad Nazim, 'Appendix L', *The Life and Times of Sultan Mahmud of Ghazna*, Cambridge University Press, 2014, pp. 207–08.
[110]Ibid.

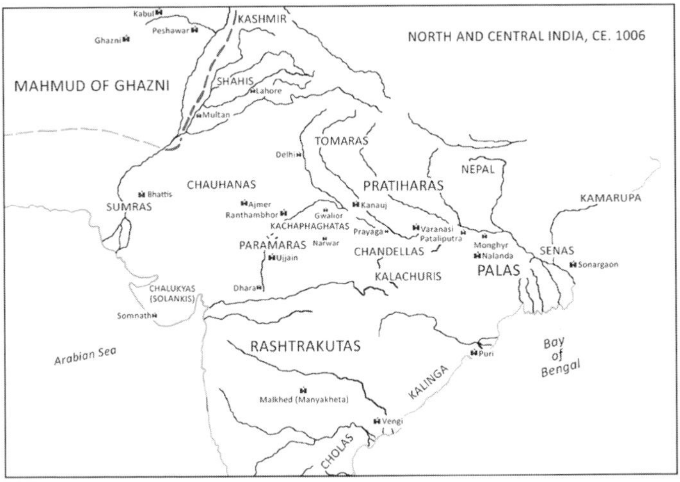

Map of north and central India, CE 1006

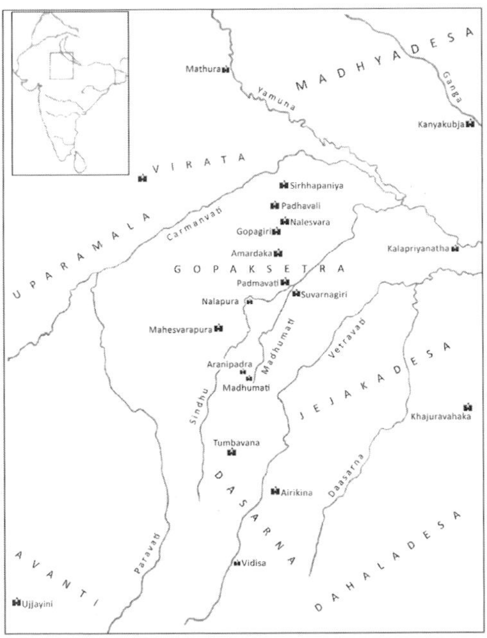

A map depicting the early medieval regions of central India

Gold coin of Gangeyadeva Vikramaditya Kalachuri

Gupta coins

Kushan coins

Silver rupee of Shivaji Holkar of Indore

Silver punch-mark coins from the Mauryan period

Silver jital, Samanta Deva, Shahis of Kabul. The reverse side (right) depicts the Nandi bull

Gold mohurs and a silver Jhar Shahi coin of Jaipur State

A view of Dausa Fort's crescent-shape hill and valleyed enclave with the modern football field at the centre

Dausa Fort wall, with a jutting tower, which would have served as a military post

One of the ancient cannons at the summit of Dausa Fort

The ancient baori within the Dausa Fort

Some early medieval pillars and carvings now built into the modern temple within the Dausa Fort complex

The Shree Surajmal Bhomiya Ji Maharaj temple, which lies at a small distance from the Dausa Fort, overlooking the maidan ground

The mysterious chabutra near the Baswa railway track that locals believe to be the final resting place of the famed Rajput warrior Rana Sanga

Chand Baori or the famous stepwell of Abhaneri

Stone carvings preserved in the gallery of Chand Baori

Madhogarth, headquarters of the Jaipur army during the battle of Tunga on 28 April 1787

Mauryan ruins dating back to the time of Ashoka at Viratnagar (Bairat)

> both occasions the sultan raised the siege on receipt of a formal submission, followed by exchange of gifts and presents, which in the hands of the Muslim chroniclers of a later period came to be depicted as 'tribute'.[111]

The peace treaty was, as customary, followed by an exchange of gifts and pleasantries. The Chandela raja is said to have composed some Hindi verses in praise of the sultan, while Mahmud is said to have sent the raja 'a robe of honour and rich presents'.[112] It would appear that there was mutual respect among the enemies, as remarks were exchanged and, in the words of Mitra, 'both sides retired with honours even'. With the exception of his failed invasion of Kashmir in 1015 CE (406 AH), this was certainly Mahmud of Ghazni's least successful campaign in his blood-soaked and battle-hardened career. Although Mahmud would return to plunder India's wealth on several more occasions, he would only choose easier pickings and never venture back to central India again after this campaign. The Bhati Jadons ruled from their capital, Lodurva, from the ninth century, and like the Kachaphaghatas, they, in 1025 CE, also had to face the depredations of Mahmud of Ghazni. Despite the constant threats of war, they retained much of their kingdom, although after the fall of Lodurva in 1152 CE, a new capital, Jaisalmer, was founded by Rawal Jaisal in 1156 CE, and remains their capital till date.

---

[111]Mitra, Sisir Kumar, *The Early Rulers of Khajuraho*, Motilal Banarsidass, Delhi, 1977, pp. 81–82.
[112]Ibid.

Aftermath of the Ghaznavid Invasion

Having successfully deflected the Ghaznavid invasion, the war, nonetheless, had an irreparable effect on the power structure of central India. From this point onwards, we find no more evidence/suggestion of the alliance between the Chandelas and the Kachaphaghatas. Although the details of what exactly transpired are unrecorded, the war with Mahmud seems to have brought to end the powerful coalition between the Chandelas and the Kachaphaghatas.[113] This, in turn, gave some breathing space to the remnants of the Pratihara power, who although much weakened were not yet wiped out.

Ultimately, this fallout led to the decline of both the Chandelas as well as Kachaphaghata powers. On one hand, the Kachaphaghatas' deadly feud with the Pratiharas would continue for another century. As for the Chandelas, they would, under Vijayapala (successor to Vidyadhara), have to contend with the expansionist policy of the Kalachuris of the Chedi kingdom. Therefore, both clans had to endure further conflicts without the aid of their former ally, which turned out to be against the interests of both the rulers of Gwalior and the lords of Kalinjar. These unsettling feuds would ultimately usher instability, hastening the decline of these early medieval Hindu states of north and central India.

---

[113]This view is supported by Mitra who states: 'The use of expressions indicative of a higher political status in respect of the Kacchapaghata king Muladeva in the Sas Bahu record, led scholars to think that the Kacchapaghata might now have disowned their alliance to the Chandellas and have become independent which , however is not impossible.' Mitra, Sisir Kumar, *The Early Rulers of Khajuraho*, Motilal Banarsidass, Delhi, 1977, p. 90.

The Pratiharas were able to exact what must have been a sweet revenge, as the Kachaphaghatas, for the final time, lost Gwalior to them in around 1129 CE.[114]

The Pratiharas' retaking of Gwalior from the Kachaphaghatas, however, was to last only for a century, as Gwalior, in 1232 CE, fell to the Delhi sultan Iltutmish, which put an end to royal Pratihara power. Nonetheless, remnants of the Pratihara dynasty did survive and settled around the pilgrimage center of Baksar (in Unnao district of Uttar Pradesh). Despite the loss of all their former royal trappings, these Pratihara descendants became known as the Ujjainiya Rajputs of Bhojpur.[115] By the early sixteenth century, they were strong enough to have become a close ally of the famed Sher Shah Suri, assisting him on his rise to power. Sher Shah Suri, while he was Sher Khan, is said to have assisted Gajpat to become leader of the Ujjainiya Rajputs. Once he became sultan, Suri is said to have conferred on Gajpat the title of 'Raja' and the districts of Rohtas and Shahabad. According to noted historian Herbert Arnold Kolff:

> Not until 1532, when Gajpat was eighteen years old, did his mother send the boys to serve her father's old ally Sher Khan, who was now building up his strength in south Bihar and who received them well. Gajpat and Bairishal now collected two thousand Ujjainiyyas and killed their rival uncle with Sher Khan's help where upon Gajput was seated on the gaddi. The Bhojpur Rajputs under

[114]Narwar, on the other hand, was lost to the rising power of the Tomar Rajputs sometime in the late twelfth century.

[115]Also known as Panwar, Pramar, Parihar or Puar Rajputs.

> Gajpat's leadership, amply repaid Sher Khan during the following tears, rendering invaluable military assistance. During the battle of Surajgarh in which Sher Khan defeated the Bengal army, he put 3,000 picked Pathans and 2,000 Ujjainiyas in his first line. The battle was won and according to the Khyat, the Bengali general was killed at the hands of Gajpat. Sher Khan was much pleased.[116]

By that time, the Kachaphaghatas, led by an able prince, had, over four centuries earlier, crossed the Chambal River and into eastern Rajasthan, and established a new principality that would eventually become the Dhundhar Raj. This prince is none other than Dūlhadeva, popularly known as Dulha Rai as well as Dhola Rao, the 'bridegroom prince'.[117]

[116]Kolff, D.H.A., *Naukar, Rajput, and Sepoy: The Ethnohistory of the Military Labour Market in Hindustan, 1450–1850*, Cambridge University Press, 2002.
[117]His popular name could be translated as bridegroom, while Rai or Rao is an early Rajput title. Thus, he is remembered as the 'bridegroom prince'.

FOUR

THE LIFE OF DULHA RAI

Dulha Rai, or the bridegroom prince, is credited with the capture of the Dausa Fort from the Meenas and the establishment of a new dynasty, the Kachwahas, who went on to rule over the area known as Dhundhar. Scant information is available on the the early period of the Dhundhar kingdom due to the lack of first-hand evidence and the differing versions of events pertaining to the life and times of Dulha Rai recorded in different texts. These issues are, firstly, the exact whereabouts of the conqueror's homeland; secondly, the nature of his conquest; and thirdly, his subsequent life.

With regards to the first issue, as shall be demonstrated below, the records of the *Kachawan Ri Vanshavali* along with the *Kachhvamsha Mahakavya* and the *Kurma Vilas* states that he was from Gwalior.[118] History records at least three branches of a clan known as Kachaphaghata who ruled over a substantial area stretching along the river Chambal, in what today comprises the state of Madhya Pradesh, during the tenth to twelfth centuries CE, with their respective capitals at Gwalior, Dubkund and Narwar. Of these, the most prominent appears to have been the branch that ruled from Gwalior between 950 CE and 1128 CE. The Sas-Bahu temple inscription of 1093 CE at Gwalior Fort lists the genealogy from Laksmana, the first of the branch of the family that ruled from Gwalior up to the reign of Mahipala, who died some time before 1104 CE. Similarly, the names of three of the rulers of the Narwar branch, Gagan Singh (r.1075–90), Sarad Singh (r. 1090–1105) and Vir Singh (r. 1105–25) are available from the Nalapur Mahadurg Grant of 1120 CE issued by King Vir Singh.[119]

It was from central India that, according to legend, Dulha Rai, a scion of the Kachaphaghata clan, came to Rajasthan. Some genealogies, besides works like the *Kachhavamsha Mahakavya* and *Kurma Vilas,* assert that 'Dhola' came from Gwalior, while writers like Nainsi, Bankidas and James Tod hold that he came from Narwar. Thus, it may be said that Dulha Rai was indeed a scion of the early medieval Kachaphaghata dynasty. It is the aim of this chapter to evaluate the conflicting angles and versions of Dulha Rai's life and achievements handed down through posterity and garner a reasonable picture of the events that led to the founding of

---

[118]Hooja, Rima, *A History of Rajasthan,* Rupa & Co., New Delhi, 2006, p. 389.

[119]Willis, Michael D., *Inscriptions of Gopaksetra: Materials for the History of Central India,* British Museum Press, 1996.

the Kachwahas and the Dhundhar kingdom. In order to do so, I shall expound the two most well-known accounts of Dulha Rai's life, these being the *Kachhawan Ri Vanshavali* and James Tod's *Annals and Antiquities of Rajasthan.*

The *Kachawan Ri Vanshavali* is among the earliest publications that contained comprehensive original text on the history of Jaipur, in Dhundhari and other Rajasthani dialects. It was intended to be used as a source material, and I have indeed found it greatly beneficial for such purpose as to demonstrate the Kachwaha's own version of the events that transpired at the founding of Dhundhar Raj and the life of Dulha Rai.

James Tod's contribution towards bringing the history and culture of the Rajputs to the English readers is a fact well known and much appreciated in India as well as abroad. Without depreciating Tod's efforts, it has been recognized in hindsight that his *Annals and Antiquities of Rajasthan*, should not be taken as authentic history. Firstly, it must be pointed out that the history he recorded from the Mughal era onwards was a fairly accurate rendition of the events that occurred and were still well-remembered and recorded by the various Rajput clans Tod encountered. The history of the period prior to that, on the other hand, being that of the early medieval period, were based solely on the bardic tales and ballads, which, despite their great heritage value, could not be relied upon as factual history. His anecdotes of the nineteenth century and outdated racial theories apart, a glaring example of Tod's inaccuracy is such that he did not recognize the former greatness of the Pratiharas.[120] Tod does at least point out that the Pratiharas were dispossessed of Mandore by Rao Chunda, who was progenitor of the Rathores in Marwar[121] as well as the fact that it was from these same Pratiharas of Mandore that the Rawals of Chittor gained the title of Rana at the beginning of the thirteenth century. These facts surely allude to the former greatness that the Pratiharas enjoyed during the early medieval period, particularly in the eighth to ninth centuries, when they acted as an effective bulwark against the initial Arab incursions into India.

In hindsight, Tod is not to be blamed for his ignorance on the matter, as the glory days of the Imperial Pratiharas has become a distant memory for almost a millennia. Understandably, Tod being a pioneer in his field, he did not get the advantage of latter-day research, which, through the translation of inscriptions and other discoveries, brought out the history of early medieval north India to a clearer extant. His interests and dedicated efforts in penning down Rajput history as he heard from the various people and bards he encountered was appreciated by the Rajputs, who considered him a friend, and he by all means reciprocated.

[120]Tod comments, 'The Parihara is scattered over Rajasthan, but I am unaware of the existence of any independent chieftainship there.' Tod, James, *Annals and Antiquities of Rajasthan*, Routledge & Kegan Paul, 1972, p. 84.

[121]Other legends state that Rao Chunda received Mandore as dowry from the Pratiharas through a matrimonial alliance, somewhat reminiscent of Dulha Rai's conquest of Dausa.

Comparative Analysis of Dulha Rai's Life Based on The Kachhawan Ri Vanshavali and James Tod's Version

Early Life and Conquest of Dausa

Firstly, we shall examine the version of events as recorded in the *Kachhawan Ri Vanshavali*, specifically Shyam Singh Ratnawat's translation of the text.

> Isha Singh, king of Gwalior, having grown old, once consulted the Brahmans as to how he could make his kingdom everlasting for his posterity. They advised him to give away the kingdom to Jai Singh, his maternal nephew, which he did. His son Sodhdev, however, continued to live at Gwalior. Later on being objected to by Jai Singh, he along with his son Dulahrai, grandson of Isha Singh, moved to village Nidravali[122]. While living there, Sodhdev wrote to Silarasi Chauhan of Pachwar, whose daughter was married to Dulahrai, requesting him to suggest some place to live in. On the advice of Silarasi, Dulahrai invaded Dausa in the guise of a caravan of horses, and in connivance with the Chauhans, who were co-partners in their passion over Dausa with the Badgujars, managed to oust the latter and get hold of the fort. The Badgujars who also ruled Deoti, again attacked Dausa but were again defeated by Dulahrai.
>
> Dulahrai then informed his father Sodhev of his victory and possession over Dausa and requested him to come with the family. Sodhdev having arrived at Dausa,

[122]In the districts of Karauli and Sawai Madhopur.

> appointed Dulahrai as his heir-apparent. Dulahrai then invaded Bhandarej and conquered it.[123]

The version of Dulha Rai's life as narrated by James Tod, which is commonly retold by recent historians, is related below:

> On the death of Sora Singh, prince of Nurwar, his brother usurped the government, depriving the infant, Dhola Rae, of his inheritance. His mother, clothing herself in mean apparel, put the infant in a basket, which she placed on her head, and travelled westward until she reached the town of Khogong (within five miles of modern Jeipoor), then inhabited by the Meenas. Distressed with hunger and fatique, she had placed her precious burthen on the ground, and was plucking some wild berries, when she observed a hooded serpent rearing its form over the basket. She uttered a shriek, which attracted an itinerant Brahmin, who told her to be under no alarm, but rather to rejoice at this certain indication of future greatness in the boy. But the emanciated parent of the founder of Amber replied, 'what may be in futurity I heed not, while I am sinking with hunger' on which the Brahmin put her in the way to Khogong, where he said her necessities would be relieved. Taking up the basket, she reached the town, which is encircled by hills, and accosting a female, who happened to be a slave of the Meena chieftain, begged

[123]Ratnawat, Shyam Singh (ed.), *Kachhawan Ri Vanshavali: A Genealogical Account of the Kacchawa Nobility,* Centre for Rajasthan Studies, University of Jaipur, Jaipur, 1981, pp. 7–8.

any menial employment for food. By direction of the Meena Rani, she was entertained with the slaves. One day she was ordered to prepare dinner, of which Ralunsi, the Meena Raja, partook, and found it so superior to his usual fare, that he sent for the cook, who related her story. As soon as the Meena chief discovered the rank of the illustrious fugitive, he adopted her as his sister, and Dhola Rae as his nephew. When the boy had attained the age of Rajpoot manhood (fourteen), he was sent to Delhi, with the tribute of Khogong, to attend instead of the Meena. The young Cuchwaha remained there five years, when he conceived the idea of usurping his benefactor's authority. Having consulted the Meena d'hadi (bard), as to the best means of executing his plan, he recommended him to take advantage of the festival of the Dewali, when it is customary to perform the ablutions en masse, in a tank. Having brought a few of his Rajpoot brethren from Delhi, he accomplished his object, filling the reservoirs in which the Meenas bathed with their dead bodies. The treacherous bard did not escape; Dhola Rae put him to death with his own hand, observing, 'he who had proved unfaithful to one master, could not be trusted by another.' He then took possession of Khogong. Soon after, he repaired to Deosah, a castle and district ruled by an independent chief of the Birgoojur tribe of Rajpoots, whose daughter he demanded in marriage. 'How can this be', said the Birgoojur, 'when we are both Suryávansi, and one hundred generations have not yet separated us?' But being convinced that the necessary number of

> descendants had intervened, the nuptials took place, and as the Birgoojur had no male issue, he resigned his power to his son-in-law.[124]

The *Kachhawan Ri Vanshavali* states that Dulha Rai, who hailed from Gwalior, invited his father to Dausa only after his complete subjugation of the fort and township, after which he utilized the strong castle of Dausa as a new base for expanding his domains westwards. This new domain became the kingdom of Dhundhar, and it was at Khoh, where 'Sodhdev' died in 1006 CE (VS 1063). On the other hand, Tod, while stating that Dulha Rai was a prince of Narwar, portrays him to be a fatherless toddler, who was indebted to the Meena Raja but then ended up, through betrayal and guile, taking over his territory.

There are more inconsistencies between the two versions of the founder's early life. The *Kachhawan Ri Vanshavali* attributes the conquest of Dausa to Dulha Rai's well-planned and well-executed stealth attack in connivance with the Chauhans, who previously ruled the area alongside the Badgurjar Rajputs[125] but wanted to utilize their new son-in-law in ousting their former allies. Tod, on the other hand, attributes Dulha Rai's rise to his cunning deception against his Meena benefactors and that he gained Dausagarh or Dausa Fort from his Badgurjar father-in-law, who was without a male heir.

---

[124]Tod, James, *Annals and Antiquities of Rajast'han, or, The Central and Western Rajpoot States of India*, Vol. 2, Smith, Elder and Co, Cornhill, Calkin and Budd, Fall Mall, 1832, pp. 347–48.

[125]Also spelled Badgujar or Bargujar.

Further, in Tod's version, the clandestine attack on Diwali occurred when the young prince was usurping the principality of Khogong, even prior to his annexation of Dausa. While on the other hand, the *Kachhawan Ri Vanshavali* does not even mention Khogong and insists that conflict with the Meenas occurred after his annexation of Dausa Fort was completed.

Conquest of Ramgarh and Jamwai Mata

Having conquered and Dausa and Bhandarej, Dulha Rai then shifted his attention to subjugating the Meena confederacy, the indigenous rulers of this area known as the Panchwara (confederacy of five). It was, however, a loose confederacy of hamlets and small forts that were not always politically united, a fact clearly recognized and exploited by Dulha Rai. There was also an existing alliance during the time between the Meenas and the Badgurjar Rajputs, who were headed by the Raja of Deoti.[126]

Below is the narration of the *Kachhawan Ri Vanshavali* on Dulha Rai's story after his possession of Dausa and Bhandarej:

> Later on he fought with the Minas at Manchi and was seriously wounded in a fierce battle. Taking Dulahrai as dead, the Minas left for Manchi and indulged in an orgy. The tutelary deity, Budhwai of the Kachhawas, appeared before Dulahrai and blessed him with victory. Dulahrai then returned to Dausa and started to attack the Minas on the next morning. The Minas were much

[126]The subjugation of the Meenas was, in fact, a multi-generation task that would be continued by Dulha Rai's descendants up until their founding of Amber.

> surprised at this and being nervous were defeated at the hands of Dulahrai. To commemorate this victory Dulahrai constructed a temple for the goddess in the valley of a hill near Manchi. He also built a fort on the hill at Manchi and changed the name of the place to Ramgarh. Dulahrai then attacked Deoti and held sway over the place by ousting the Badgujars. Next, he killed Chanda Mina of Khoh, Geta Mina of Getore and shifted his residence to Khoh from Dausa. It was at Khoh that Sodhdev expired in the year VS. 1063 (1006 AD).[127]

According to Tod's version: 'With the additional means thus at his disposal, Dhola determined to subjugate the Seroh tribe of Meenas, whose chief, Rao Natto, dwelt at Mauch. Again he was victorious, and deeming his new conquest better adapted for a residence than Khogong, he transferred his infant government tither, changing the name of Mauch, in honour of his great ancestor, to Ramgurh.'[128]

It was during this particular episode of his struggle against the Meenas that Jamwai Mata (of Ramgarh) came to be the kuldevi of the Kachwahas in Dhundhar. There are, of course, several versions of the story, although these could basically be divided into the Meena's version or the Rajput's version, but both concur that Manchi (Mauch) was captured and renamed

[127]Ratnawat, Shyam Singh (ed.), *Kachhawan Ri Vanshavali: A Genealogical Account of the Kacchawa Nobility,* Centre for Rajasthan Studies, University of Jaipur, Jaipur, 1981, pp. 7–8.

[128]Tod, James, *Annals and Antiquities of Rajast'han, or, The Central and Western Rajpoot States of India*, Vol 2, Smith, Elder and Co, Cornhill, Calkin and Budd, Fall Mall, 1832.

by the conqueror to Ramgarh. Dulha Rai must have done so in honour of his august ancestor as well as to justify the dharmic nature of his enterprise. With regards to the differences between the two versions, it must be noted that Tod's version does not mention the first failed attempt to subjugate the Meenas of Mauch, whereas this issue is highlighted in the *Kachhawan Ri Vanshavali*, as it is the reason that the kuldevi of the Kachwahas in Dhundhar came into being.

Another glaring difference is that while according to the version championed by Tod, Dulha Rai's last conquest was Mauch, the *Kachhawan Ri Vanshavali*, on the other hand, goes into further detail on the defeat of the Badgurjar raja of Deoti, which was deemed worthy of remembrance. Additionally, the *Kachhawan Ri Vanshavali* states that Dulha Rai subsequently defeated the Chanda Meenas of Khoh (6 miles east of modern Jaipur), and made the place his forward base of operation. This led next to his assault on the Ghaita Meenas, who bravely defended their territory but were defeated, and as a result, the area that is presently known as Gaitore, which derives its name from this clan of Meenas, was added to Dulha Rai's territory (the area of present-day Jaipur was all but jungle and sand dunes at that time).

The Death of Dulha Rai

The *Kachhawan Ri Vanshavali* decribes Dulha Rai's twilight years in so many words:

> Dulahrai, having been crowned as king, left for Gwalior, on a request from there, to fight with the enemy who had come from the Deccan. Though Dulahrai succeeded

> in liquidating the enemy, he got several wounds which resulted in his death on his return to Khoh in the year V.S. 1093 (1036 AD). He had two sons, one Kakil who was crowned after him and the other Vikal whose Progeny known as Vikalpota settled at Lahar, Rampur etc.[129]

On the other hand, according to James Tod:

> Dhola subsequently married the daughter of the prince of Ajmer, whose name was Maroni. Returning on one occasion with her from visiting the shrine of Jumwahi Mata, the whole force of the Meenas of that region assembled, to the number of eleven thousand, to oppose his passage through their country. Dhola gave them battle; but after slaying vast numbers of his foes, he was himself killed and his followers fled. Maroni escaped, and bore a posthumous child, who was named Kankul, and who conquered the country of Dhoondar. His son, Maidul Rao, made a conquest of Amber from the Soosawut Meena confederation. He also subdued the Nandhla Meenas, and added the district of Gatoor-Gatti to his territory.[130]

The *Kachhawan Ri Vanshavali* attributes the downfall of Dulha Rai to be a result of injuries succumbed by fighting

---

[129]Ratnawat, Shyam Singh (ed.), *Kachhawan Ri Vanshavali: A Genealogical Account of the Kacchawa Nobility,* Centre for Rajasthan Studies, University of Jaipur, Jaipur, 1981, pp. 7–8.

[130]Tod, James, *Annals and Antiquities of Rajast'han, or, The Central and Western Rajpoot States of India,* Vol 2, Smith, Elder and Co, Cornhill, Calkin and Budd, Fall Mall, 1832.

enemies from the 'Deccan' and not the Meenas, having liquidated the enemy, he is said to have died on his return to Khoh. Upon examination of the early history of the Kachwahas in Chapter 3, we know that during the second and third decades of the eleventh century, the fortunes of the Kachaphaghatas, having deflected the Ghaznavid onslaught in 1022 CE, and with the weakening of the Chandelas (now under the rule of Vijayapala, successor to Vidyadhara), was on the rise. However, the constant fog of war smouldered on, and like the Chandelas, they seemed to have been in conflict against invaders from the southern border, this time being the Chedi kingdom (the Kalachuris of Tripuri). It is acknowledged by many sources that the Kalachuris, under the leadership of their greatest king, Gangeyadeva (r. 1015–41 CE), made concerted expansion efforts northwards. Gangeyadeva's forces are said to have won victories against the kings of Kira, Anga, Kuntala and Utkala. According to the historian Sisir Kumar Mitra, the Daob region was under the firm grip of the Chandelas up till the time of Vidyadhara, therefore, the northwards expansion of the Kalachuris must have been achieved at the cost of the Chandelas.[131] Therefore, taking in mind Gangeyadeva's aggressive campaigns in north India, there is, after all, a grain of truth in the cause of death attributed to Dhola Rai in the KV.

James Tod's version, on the other hand, simply states that he died while fighting the Meenas upon his departure from

[131]Mitra, Sisir Kumar, *The Early Rulers of Khajuraho*, Motilal Banarsidass, Delhi, 1977, p. 89.

Ramgarh, and that his wife, Maroni, was carrying his unborn child at the time, who was born later and came to be known as Konkul (Kakildeva). Tod's oversimplification of Dulha Rai's death highlights his lack of knowledge with regards the founder's connection with his birthplace as well as the fact that Dulha Rai is recorded to have had two sons, Kakildeva and Vikalji, in the genealogical records of the Kachwahas.[132] There is also a version that states that Dulha Rai died while fighting on the side of his Tomara cousins of Gwalior; however, the Tomaras did not capture Gwalior until 1398, which was long after Dulha Rai's time, so this version must be discounted. This belief likely arose due to a confusion in the early history of the clan as well as the fact that the Tomaras were the Rajputs who, at a later period, came to be associated with Gwalior for many centuries.

Now that the early history of the Kachwahas has been illuminated, there appears to be more credit in the version of Dulha Rai's death as recorded in the *Kachhawan Ri Vanshavali* than that of James Tod's version. In hindsight, it is now recognized that Gwalior was, in fact, the main seat of power for his family at the time, while Dausa was a newly added principality to the Kachaphaghata's dominion. In the previous chapter it has also been pointed out that between 1018 and 1022 CE, there was a recorded victory of the Kachaphaghatas against the forces of Malwa, who attempted to invade Gopaksetra. It could be seen that this recorded conflict with the Paramaras took place about 16

[132]Singh Dunlod, Harnath, *Geneological Table of the Kachhawahas,* Navneet Art Printers, Jaipur.

years prior to the recorded death of Dulha Rai; therefore, the conflict in which he fought and sustained injury must have been the war with the Kalachuris, which, according to the *Kachhawan Ri Vanshavali*, was the last campaign Dulha Rai was involved with, before succumbing to his wounds on the way back to Khoh. It is most probable that Dulha Rai was called by his clansmen to Gwalior to fight under the Kachaphaghata banner against the Kalachuri invaders. The *Kachhawan Ri Vanshavali* recorded that he was wounded from this conflict and died on the way back to his capital at Khoh. The fact that he died on his return to Khoh may have given rise to oral tradition of a surprise attack from the Meenas, which James Tod recorded.

Matrimony and Family

Here, it should be clarified that while in Tod's version Dulha Rai is said to have been married to a Badgurjar princess, the *Kachhawan Ri Vanshavali* asserts that he was married to a Chauhan princess. The compromised truth seems to be that he was married to both, the first marriage is certainly the turning point, which drew him into the area, and the second marriage was the result of his wresting control of the Dausa Fort from the Badgurjars, which led him into conflict with the Raja of Deoti, head of the Badgurjars.

This point is concurred by Rima Hooja, who states that it was not improbable that Dulha Rai eventually married the daughters of both the locally prominent Chauhan and Badgurjar chiefs, and it was after the sealing of these alliances that he set his eyes on neighbouring territories, which were held by the various indigenous Meena chiefs.[133]

It may be said that in order to make peace with the Badgurjars and stabilize his infant acquisition, he cemented this new conquest through his second marriage. The name of his second Badgurjar consort has, however, been lost. Perhaps one of these ranis had the popular nickname of Maroni, which is romantically remembered by later generations and bardic ballads as the spouse of Dulha Rai.[134]

Dulha Rai is said to have had two sons, Kakildeva and Vikalji (alternatively spelt as Bikal). Kakildeva, Dulhai Rai's firstborn from his Chauhan rani, a hardened warrior, must have spent much of his time in Dausa Fort and Bhandarej. Possibly holding the fort (literally) when he was not out on a campaign with his father, who having secured Dausa and Bhandarej, was out on a campaign to capture Muach from its then Meena overlord.

As Kakildeva's descendents inherited the gaddi of the newly founded Dhundhar Raj, Dulha Rai's descendants came to be known as 'Bhai Beta' within the clan structure of the Kachwahas of Dhundhar.[135]

On the other hand, the descendants of Vikalji became known as 'Vikalpota' and settled at Lahar, Rampura, Gopalpura, Khakhsis, Khedi, Sundar, Kalsada, Sarssodo, Bhoroli, Mohino, Machand and Belo in Madhya Pradesh.[136]

---

[133]Hooja, Rima, *A History of Rajasthan*, Rupa & Co., New Delhi, 2006, p. 394.

[134]This may also be due to the widespread confusion between Dhola of the Dhola-Maru folktale with Dulha Rai.

[135]The Ganayats, on the other hand, were the nobles of other Rajput clans that were related to the chieftain through matrimonial alliances.

[136]Singh Dunlod, Harnath, *Geneological Table of the Kachhawahas,* Navneet

According to A. H. Bingley, 'The Kachwaha of Bulandshahr state that their ancestors migrated from Narwar to Amber and thence to the Doab. The Raja of Rampur in Jalaun is the head of the clan in the North-west.'[137]

It should be pointed out that the Kachwahas in Uttar Pradesh as well as Madhya Pradesh are the descendants of Vikalji, second son of Dulha Rai, and their very existence alone testifies to the fact that Dulha Rai's lineage enjoyed an intimate connection with his ancestral domain of Gwalior, Narwar and the surrounding Doab.

When concerned with this early history of the Dhundhar Raj, with scant surviving recorded details, a picture about the policies and alliances of the state could be glanced from the matrimonial alliances sanctioned. After all, diplomatic relations and the forming of offensive/defensive networks was an integral part of the state's survival in those politically volatile and turbulent ages.

It is, therefore, vital to note that matrimonial alliances with the Chauhans were further cemented by Dulha Rai's son Kakildeva, who married two Chauhan princesses, one being Kumkum Devi, daughter of Jetsi of Moran (his mother's cousin) and the other being the daughter of the Raja of Ranthambore, his powerful neighbour to the south-east.

Art Printers, Jaipur, p. 10; Ratnawat, Shyam Singh (ed.), *Kachhawan Ri Vanshavali (A Genealogical Account of the Kacchawa Nobility)*, Centre for Rajasthan Studies, University of Jaipur, Jaipur, 1981, p. 190.

[137]Bingley, A.H., *Handbook on Rajputs*, Asian Educational Services, New Delhi, 1996, p. 89.

Conquest of Dausa

Another confusing aspect of Dulha Rai's life is the exact date on which he began his westward foray into Rajasthan. According to genealogical tables in the Jaipur archives, the date (according to the Hindu calendar) of his father's (Sodhadeva/Sodha Singh) accession is given as Kartik Vadi 10, S.1023 (966 CE), while the date for Dulha Rai's accession is given as Magha Sudi 7, S.1063 (1006 CE). The Jaipur Khyat, on the other hand, gives a similar date of Magha Sudi 6, S.1063 as Dulha Rai's date of accession.[138] Thus, the two records of his accession date matches, with just a one-day difference.

Interestingly, the year 967 CE is speculated by many sources to be the year of Dulha Rai's shift to Dausa. According to Giles Tillotson, 'Soon after Amber had been founded by Mina Tribesmen early in the tenth century, the Kachwaha Rajputs (who had previously ruled in Gwalior established themselves in an adjacent region, founding Dhundhar as their capital in 967 CE.'[139]

The date of Sodhadeva is contemporary to the time of Laksamana Kachchaphaghata, who may have been the head of the family ruling at Gwalior. Even during the reigns of Vajradama as well as Mangalaraja, it must be noted that the Kachaphaghatas were branching out and capturing new

[138]Sarkar, Jadunath, *A History of Jaipur c. 1503–1938*, Raghubir Sinh (ed.), Orient Longman, 1984; Ratnawat, Shyam Singh (ed.), *Kachhawan Ri Vanshavali: A Genealogical Account of the Kacchawa Nobility*, Centre for Rajasthan Studies, University of Jaipur, Jaipur, 1981.

[139]Tillotson, Giles, *The Rajput Palaces: The Development of an Architectural Style 1450–1750*, Oxford University Press, 1999, p. 88.

territories in different directions. Referring to the Dubkund branch of the Kachaphaghatas, epigraphic evidence records the name of Yuvaraja to have ruled there during the year 1000 CE. Historian Ahmed Ali comments:

> The rulers of Dubkunda branch of the Kachaphaghatas were immigrants of Suhanai (Sihonia). H.N. Dwivedi has also traced out their migration from Suhania. It was when Vajradamana defeated the (Pratihara) king of Gandhinagara, he shifted his seat of power to Gwalior and later on some members of the family migrated go Dubkunda. Thus the rulers of this branch were related to the family of Laksmana.[140]

It could be seen that the spreading out of Kachaphaghatas from their ancestral domain of Gopaksetra from the mid-tenth and early eleventh centuries is a concrete fact and not mere speculation. Dulha Rai's conquest of Dausa should, therefore, be understood as the branching out of Kachaphaghatas during this era of expansion and consolidation. It must also be added that the meaning of Yuvaraja, who is said to have ruled at Dubkund is, of course, translated as 'crown prince'; therefore, one wonders whether this name recorded was his title rather than his name. The Dubkund branch of the Kachaphaghatas ruled the area for over 200 years until the beginning of the twelfth century, when they were displaced by another power. It must be noted, however, that the dates presented are not totally without dispute, as Cunningham suggests 1128–29 CE

[140]Ali, Ahmed, *Kachchhapaghata Art and Architecture*, Publication Scheme, Jaipur, 2005, p. 4.

as the date of Dulha Rai's conquest of Dausa and its adjoining districts. Cunningham's date would make sense if, indeed, Sodhadeva is identified with Madhusudana of the Gwalior branch of the Kachaphaghatas, and Dulha Rai is none other than Tejkarana, who was the last known ruler of this branch. Cunningham's view is supported by Rai Bahadur Ram Saini and Ahmed Ali.

Additional Information Handed Down Through Posterity

By stroke of luck, I was able to obtain additional information regarding this episode of Dhundhar's founding history by a person whose ancestor was directly related to the events narrated above. Dr Subanshu Gayawala, chancellor of Suresh Gyan Vihar University, was kind enough to inform me of the tales passed down from his ancestors for over a millennia, and also the reason he gained his unique family name. According to Dr Gayawala, it was after consulting with his advisors, (who according to Tod were the Meena bards) that Dulha Rai decided to attack the Meenas of Mauch on the second day of DulhaDiwali. Till date, it is still a custom in the Jaipur court to wear black on Diwali to commemorate this event. There are two explanation as to the tradition of black being worn on Diwali, the first being to mourn the Meenas, who were killed importunately, and the second is that black was the colour of camouflage used during the night attack.

After Dulha Rai's first failed attempt of conquest against the Meenas of Mauch, he was left for dead on the field of battle, Dr Gayawala narrates:

> Dholarai having been left for dead, some Brahmins living in the area came to survey the scene of battle. At that moment a cow appeared and dropped milk on to Dulharai's body and miraculously healed him. Having been healed he got up and put his hands together in reverence towards the cow. At that instant the cow transformed into the form of the goddess and told Dulharai that earlier she was known as Budhwai mata, and she was the mother goddess of his family. However, from today onwards, due to enterprises that lay ahead for his family, she would hence be known as Jamwai mata.[141]

Henceforth, it was a tradition in the Kachwaha royal court to maintain a cow in the royal palace. This duty was indeed assigned to Dr Subanshu Gayawala's ancestor, who had his chance encounter with Dulha Rai during this particular episode. This tradition continued uninterrupted as the Kachwaha capital moved, several times in the following centuries, and was discontinued only in 1923 during my grandfather's reign, due to his constant travels and work, which kept him away from Jaipur more than his immediate predecessors. It is also how Dr Subanshu's family earned the unique name 'Gayawala'.

He also added that this may have been due to the supernatural need to counter against the shakti (power) of Bakhi Mata, revered by the local population. Therefore, this story handed down through posterity points out that Dulha Rai was able to turn around what seemed like defeat

[141]Cunningham, A., *Archaeolgical Survey of India Report*, Vol. II, p. 319; Bhatnagar, V.S., *Life and Times of Sawai Jai Singh 1688–1743*, Impex India, Delhi, 1974.

into a surprise victory. This miraculous feat was achieved after he experienced an epiphany, which led to his increased devotion towards the goddess who came to be known as Jamwai Mata, the Kuldevi of the Kachwahas in Dhundhar.

The Confusion between Dhola of Narwar and Dulha Rai

One outstanding issue that needs to be addressed with regards to Dulha Rai's history is the long-standing confusion between the founder of the Dhundhar Raj and the Dhola of the Dhola–Maru fame. This confusion is somewhat understandable as both characters are similarly remembered fondly as Dhola/ Dulha Rai. Both are Raghuvanshis and are said to be from Narwar. However, while the Kachaphaghatas can stake the claim of being the founders of Gwalior, Narwar appears to be a much older settlement, being mentioned in nothing less than the Mahabharata, as well as the *Naishadha Charita* epic.

The bardic epic of Dhola–Maru has been dated by experts to the sixteenth century, and appears to be a sequel of the older well-known Braj oral epic of Raja Nala and Damayanti (Dumenti). In Dhola–Maru, Raja Nala and Damayanti have a son named Dhola who is married to Maru (Maruni), daughter of Raja Budh Singh of Marwar (Pingal). The story has many different versions in different tongues, and it would be a near impossible task to recount them all. Suffice to say that the confusion between Dhola and Dulha Rai is increased by the fact that none other than James Tod himself believed the two characters to be one and the same. As already pointed out, Tod's account should not be taken as authentic history.

With regards to the confusion between Dhola and Dulha Rai, Dr Dasharatha Sharma points that Tod did not know that 'Dhola Rae' and 'Dulha Rae' were two different persons and that Dhola was the ancestor of Vajradaman Kachaphghata of Gwalior, while the other (Dulha Rai) was his descendent.[142]

Rima Hooja also observes this common misunderstanding and states that Tod viewed 'Dhola', who is remembered in the Dhola–Maru ballads as having married Maroni, daughter of the ruler of Ajmer, to be identical with 'Dulha Rai' who established the Kachwaha rule in Dhundhar, and that this common folk belief has persisted till the present.[143]

In fact, as demonstrated by Dr Sharma, Dhola is, according to *Nainsi Ri Khyat,* believed to have been an early ancestor of Dulha Rai and certainly not one and the same character.

It is likely that Dhola of the Dhola–Maru fame was an early Kachaphaghata prince who was descended from Suraj Sen, founder of Gwalior. There is a list compiled in 1931 which points to this.[144] This list compiled by Thakur Vir Singh Tanwar, head of Alwar State's historical research section, presents a genealogical line of rulers after Suraj Sen for 20 generations until the name of the famed Raja Nala of Narwar:

---

[142]Sharma, Dasharatha, *Rajasthan Through the Ages,* Vol. 1, Rajasthan State Archives, Bikaner, 1966, p. 693.

[143]Hooja, Rima, *A History of Rajasthan,* Rupa & Co., New Delhi, 2006, p. 390.

[144]Nath, Aman, *Jaipur: The Last Destination,* India Book House, 1996.

Surya Sen

Palandev

Rakshpal

Padmpal

Bhimpal

Nandpal

Vijaypal

Vishnupal

Dhundhpal

Krishnapal

Gyanpal (Gonantpal)

Sangrampal

Padmpal

Dharmpal

Rampal

Turatpal

Shoorpal

Shankarpal

Kishanpal

Gotampal

Nala

In conclusion, it is known that Dhola, son of Raja Nala of Narwar, through his deeds of romantic endeavour and prowess achieved legendary status and was henceforth remembered and popularized by bards through the millennia. Nevertheless, there is a need to point out that Dhola of the Dhola–Maru epic and Dulha Rai, the founder of Dhundhar, are by all practical means separate personalities. Equally important is that one appears to be an ancestor of the other. This also possibly points to the fact that while the epigraphic records of the early Kachaphaghatas of Narwar did not survive to our time, however, some of their rulers such as Raja Nala and his son Dhola were prominent enough to have been remembered and sang about by bards in both Braj bhasa and Rajasthani tongues.

Assimilation of the Meenas into the Dhundhar Raj

It must be pointed out that it was the ingenious effort of Dulha Rai and his immediate descendants that the relationship between the Kachwahas and the Meenas is that of a cordial and cooperative nature, and both communities coexist in harmony and respect one another. As a means of absorbing the aboriginal Meenas into their state, the early rulers of Dhundhar granted land rights and estates to the Meena chieftains in accordance to their rank and honour, much of which was held in hereditary succession. Furthermore, the vigour and ability of the Meenas were utilized, as the tribe became sentinels and fierce watchmen of Dhundhar's most important strongholds, such as Jaigarh and Nahargarh, while many also entered the police force. As a matter of fact, the chieftain of the Meenas was given the high honour of anointing the new rulers of Amber at the coronation ceremony, as Sir Jadunath Sarkar narrates:

> Even the tika or red mark on the forehead of every Amber-Jaipur raja at his coronation was originally made by the leader of the Minas, with blood drawn out of his big toe. But when the Mughal emperors themselves agreed to anoint the new Kachwaha rajahs with their own hands (in sandal paste), this function of the Mina headman was discontinued.[145]

This was the unique position that the Meenas held until the absorption of Jaipur State into the Indian Union. Today, the aboriginal Meenas of yesteryears are a successful community of Rajasthan, branching of into many fields, from business to politics, while many are still employed by the (current) state as police and soldiers, in a manner similar to how their ancestors served during the time of the Dhundhar Raj.

Conclusion

Thus having studied the history of the Kachaphaghatas in the previous chapter, and the two main versions of Dulha Rai's life, we have been able to construct a trajectory of the events that possibly unfolded a millennia earlier. I am, perhaps naturally, more inclined towards the version recorded by the *Kachhawan Ri Vanshavali* than James Tod's version, which is

---

[145]Sarkar, Jadunath, *A History of Jaipur c. 1503–1938*, Raghubir Sinh (ed.), Orient Longman, New Delhi, 1984, p. 12.

a compilation of rumours and stories picked up on his travels through the region and is today often believed to be a true account of the past events by unsuspecting readers.

While the two sources disagree with regards to his early life and the nature/methods of his conquest, there are two major points that are unanimously agreed upon by both sources. Firstly, the fact that he was able to subjugate the Meenas of Mauch and changed its name to Ramgarh, where he built the temple of Jamwai Mata and constructed fortifications. Secondly, that he shifted his residence from Dausa to Khoh.

It was at Khoh that, according to the *Kachhawan Ri Vanshavali*, 'Sodheva' or Sodhadeva, the father of Dulha Rai, expired in the year 1006 CE (VS 1063). Thus, the young bridegroom prince became a ruler in his own right. On the other hand, in Tod's version, 'Sora Singh' died when Dulha Rai was an infant and was, thus, robbed of his rightful rule of Gwalior by his uncle. This is another issue that brings doubt to the authenticity of Tod's version, which states that the young Dulha Rai, upon reaching manhood, was sent by his Meena benefactor as an ambassador of Khogong to present tribute to the rulers of Delhi.[146] Delhi, during early eleventh century, was under the control of the Tomara Rajputs; however, its political importance over eastern Rajasthan during the period would have been negligible in comparison to neighbouring centers of power such as Ranthambore,

[146]None other than Jadunath Sarkar himself concurs that Tod's version of events is full of fanciful accounts and is full of biases towards the house of Jaipur; Sarkar, Jadunath, *A History of Jaipur c. 1503–1938*, Raghubir Sinh (ed.), Orient Longman, 1984.

Ujjain, Gwalior or Kannauj. This is coupled with the fact that there are no known oral or written records concerning the Meenas of eastern Rajasthan and their relationship/alliance with the Tomaras of Delhi. It seems quite likely that this version of events was made up a few centuries after Dulha Rai completed his conquest, by which time, Delhi rose up to become politically important, with the inception of the Delhi sultanate at the beginning of the thirteenth century.

It must be remembered that the story of Dulha Rai's rise to power spans the period from late tenth to the early eleventh centuries, during which time the leading powers of north India, namely the Paramaras, Pratiharas, Chauhans and Chandelas, were vying for power amidst the backdrop of invasions from the north (Ghaznavid) as well as the south (the Kalachuris). It is also now clear that it was due to Dulha Rai's eastwards expansion that by the mid-twelfth century, as the power of the Kachaphaghatas in Gopaksetra began to falter, the Kurmas of Dhundhar grew in strength to become a kingdom in their own right. In this regard, despite a short period during which Dausa served as capital, it was indeed the springboard or stepping stone for the emergence of this royal branch of the Kurmas, etching their name in the history of Rajasthan and the annals of Indian history. At that point in time, amidst the turbulent background of constantly shifting political boundaries, the annexation of Dausa into Kachaphaghata control and the founding of Dhundhar Raj may have been seen as an inconsequential detail. However, within a matter of a century or two, many of the great powers whose names were revered in the eleventh century almost completely vanished from the scene. Time devours everything, empires and egos that once thought themselves invincible all but vanished into thin air, while the seemingly inconsequential annexation by Dulha Rai turned out to have had a great impact on Indian history in the following centuries. The Kachaphaghatas/Kurmbas/Kurmas were able to survive this violent and turbulent age, thanks undoubtedly to the ingenious effort of their prodigal son, the bridegroom prince—Dulha Rai.

FIVE

A BRIEF HISTORY OF DAUSA

The district of Dausa, which lies in north-east Rajasthan, is approximately 56 kilometres east of Jaipur on the main highway to Agra. Dausa's border touches Alwar to the north, Jaipur to the west, Tonk to its south-west, Sawai Madhopur to the south, while Bharatpur and Karauli lies to its east. It is the site of an ancient township also named Dausa, derived from the Sanskrit Devansa or Daivasa. It is from Dausa that the Kachwaha clan of Rajputs, founded by Dulha Rai, began their long and arduous ascension to become one of the major kingdoms of Rajputana. Despite the fact that the district of Dausa gained its name from this ancient township and its significant historical connection to the Kachwaha clan, the fort of Dausa remains a seldom-visited site by outsiders.

It must be admitted that no first-hand material survives from the period in which Dausa served as the capital of Dhundhar, apart from the walls, bricks, mortars and baoris themselves. It is a period which is closer to what historians today refer to as 'early medieval India', which unlike the late medieval period was not yet influenced by Persian culture, known for their fondness of recording written history with exact chronology and in minute detail. However, based on archaeological surveys and records of later periods, it is possible to provide a brief background of this fascinating locality in eastern Rajasthan.

Vedic and Ancient Period

The first epigraphic record of Dausa surfaces from the period of the Imperial Pratiharas, and it is from then on that there is a clear picture of the district's history. However, a brief examination of the political environs of the area throughout the ages will help us gain a broader view of Dausa's past.

Much of the area covering the erstwhile Jaipur princely state, particularly its north-eastern portion as well as the areas forming Alwar, Bharatpur as well as Dholpur, Karauli and Dausa was known in Vedic times as Matsyadesha or Madhyadesa. Matsya is often literally translated as 'fish', although it is also known by other ancient sources as the 'the middle kingdom', being the land more or less situated in the middle of the Indian subcontinent.

The kingdom of Matsya was, by the sixth century BCE, one of the 16 mahajanapadas (great states)[147] of ancient

[147]The 16 mahajanapadas were Kamboja, Gandhara, Kuru, Surasena, Matsya, Avanti, Assaka, Panchala, Chedi, Vatsa, Kosala, Kashi, Malla, Vajji, Magadha and Anga (Vanga).

India, according to the Rig Veda, the Kaushtiki Upanishad and the Buddhist Anguttara Nikaya.[148] During this period, Matsyadesha was bordered by the Surasena to its east, Vatsa and Chedi to its south-east, and Avanti to its south.

Its initial capital is believed to have been Upaplavya, although the exact location of this site has long been lost to the mist of time. According to the Shatapatha Brahmana, the Matsya king Dhavasan Dvaitavana was powerful enough to perform the ashvamedha yajna or the Vedic horse sacrifice.

During the age of the Mahabharata, the capital of this long-forgotten Matsya kingdom was Viratanagari or Viratnagar (present-day Bairat township in Jaipur district). The ancient name of Viratanagari is, in fact, an affirmation to the association of this area in eastern Rajasthan to the Mahabharata, as it was the capital city of the epic ruler of Matsyadesha, King Virata, who gave refuge to the five Pandava brothers and their wife Draupadi for 13 years when they were on exile incognito. There is, indeed, a hill known as the Bhimji ki Dungri or Bhemsen Doongri at a distance of one mile north-east of Bairat, which is situated near a cave that is believed to be associated with Bhima, the second Pandava brother.[149] Additionally, it is here that Kichika (Keechak) was killed by Bhima.

Eventually, the area later became part of the Surasena kingdom, with its capital at Mathura, the famed ancient centre of knowledge and culture located near the western

---

[148]Hooja, Rima, *A History of Rajasthan*, Rupa & Co., New Delhi, 2006, p. 94.
[149]Sahni, Daya Ram, Rai Bahadur, *Excavations at Bairat,* Publication Scheme, Jaipur, 1999, p. 24.

Uttar Pradesh/eastern Rajasthan border.

By the time of the Mauryan emperor Ashoka the Great, Matsya kingdom, along with much of the subcontinent, was under the consolidated rule of Pataliputra, the imperial capital of Magadha. Viratnagar, though, was still an important city that not only exerted control over north-eastern Rajasthan but even had personal connections with Ashoka the Great.

According to Dr Dasharatha Sharma, the areas of Bairat and Lalsot and Rairh was, from the centuries preceding the Christian Era up until the sixth century, strongly entrenched in Buddhism.[150] This is amply evident from the remains of Mauryan Buddhist archaeological sites in Bairat—the hilltop Mauryan Buddhist monastery, emperor Ashoka's Bairat Rock Edict, as well as a circular temple believed to be one of the earliest-known Buddhist stupas.[151] At Bhabru, 12 miles from Bairat, there was also discovered the only known Ashokan stone slab inscription (sila-phalaka) known as the Bhabru Rock Edict. One Captain Burtis is credited with discovering the stone slab in 1840, and it is now homed at the museum of the Asiatic Society in Kolkata. This is also perhaps a testament that during ancient times, the settlements at Viratnagar was much more extensive than the isolation and tranquility that greets visitors today.[152]

Mathura then rose to power when it became the eastern capital of the Kushan Empire during the time of the

[150]Sharma, Dasharatha, *Rajasthan Through the Ages*, Vol. 1, Rajasthan State Archives, Bikaner, 1966, pp. 57–58.

[151]It is, in fact, said to be an Ashokan 'proto-stupa'.

[152]The translations of both the rock edicts are given in Appendix III.

great emperor Kanishka (r. 127–50 CE), and thus exerted its influence into eastern Rajasthan up until around the mid-fourth century.

Following the fall of the Kushan Empire, much of Rajasthan, but particularly eastern Rajasthan, was said to have been under the control of powerful Naga confederacies. Historian Rima Hooja suggests that there were many states, both monarchic and republican, in Rajasthan and central India that were for a while united under the leadership of Ganapati Naga, with his famed center of power at Padmavati in Gopaksetra (in modern Madhya Pradesh) as well as Narwar and Mathura (now under Naga rule). Other townships associated with the Nagas were Nagaur, Nagda, Mandore and Toda Raisingh, among others.[153]

Gupta influence in Rajasthan is believed to have indirectly increased from the time of Emperor Samudragupta (r. 335–75 CE) onwards. Gupta hegemony, however, was disrupted with the invasion of the Hunas in the sixth century CE, during which time the Buddhist sites at Bairat and throughout the region are believed to have been desecrated by the barbaric forces of the Huna king Mihirakula. This belief is based on the observation of the Chinese monk Xuanzang, who recorded that the Buddhist monasteries of Gandhara were destroyed while its population was put to the sword by the forces of Mihirakula.

The fact that the Alkhon Huns reached into central India and eastern Rajasthan is accepted, although they were overthrown within a matter of decades (as explored

[153]Hooja, Rima, *A History of Rajasthan*, Rupa & Co., 2006, p. 162.

in Chapter 2). The fall of the Imperial Guptas dramatically changed the political landscape of north India. According to Dasharatha Sharma, with regards the administrative setup during the Gupta period, as far as Rajasthan is concerned, there was a shift of power from the centre to the republics that existed in the region under Gupta sovereignty. After the death of Skandagupta, Rajasthan became divided into a number of small states.[154]

Sharma notes, Bairat was, in 641 CE, under a Vaishya ruler who was a brave, impetuos and very warlike.[155] Rima Hooja hypothesizes that Naga political influence in Rajasthan began to decline by the end of the eighth century and it is likely that it was from this period onwards that they were absorbed into the emerging Rajput polity.[156] This is supported by the fact that the eighth century is also the period in which the world-renowned Chand Baori and the Vaishnavite temple today known as the Harshatmata temple of Abhaneri (ancient Abhanagari), were constructed by the Nikhumbha Rajputs.

During this period, many other centers of powers also emerged in other parts of Rajasthan, such as Shakambari or Mandore. However, in relation to eastern Rajasthan, while Mathura remained an important center of trade and learning,

---

[154]Sharma, Dasharatha, *Rajasthan Through the Ages*, Vol. I, Rajasthan State Archives, Bikaner, 1966, p. 69.

[155]Ibid. 101.

[156]Hooja, Rima, *A History of Rajasthan*, Rupa & Co., 2006, p. 202; Dasharatha Sharma also suggests there was a linkage between the emergence of the Chauhans of Shakambari and Nadol with the Nagas of Ahichchhatrapura.

the area witnessed the rise of the Chauhan Sapadalaksha kingdom. Even more importantly, in the following centuries, the center of power that arose to dominate the whole of northern and central India, including eastern Rajasthan, was Kannauj, the famed imperial capital of Pushyabhuti ruler Harshavardhana.

As the influence of Buddhism in eastern Rajasthan declined, it is interesting to note that Abhaneri, during this period, became associated with Jainism. Abhaneri's deep association with Jainism is said to have been induced by the patronage of rich merchants inhabiting the area who contributed towards the construction and maintenance of Jain temples, more noticeably the two Jain temples that were dedicated to lord Adinatha and Mahavira. These two temples were also well-known in earlier times. A merchant named Desala and his son Jaga lived at this place and had spent their wealth in charities during famines. Jain pattavalis record that there were several temples with high sikharas and rest houses in the region. The sculptural survey proves that Jainism flourished at Abhaneri between the eighth and tenth centuries AD. There is an idol of Mahavira enshrined in a small room near the entrance of Harshatmata temple that is now worshipped as Hanuman. A fragmentary piece of Jain sculpture depicting a Tirthankara image and a pedestal have also been found in Chand Baori.[157]

By the ninth century, much of north-western and central India was under the sway of the Imperial Pratiharas.

[157]Yadav, Rajendra, *Sculptural Art of Abaneri: A Paradigm*, Jawahar Kala Kendra, Jaipur, 2006, p. 3.

Initially, their capital was at Bhinmal, followed by Mandore in Rajasthan; however, as their power expanded eastwards, they captured the royal metropolis of Kannauj and made it their capital. The first epigraphic inscription relating to Dausa as a settlement dates from this period.

Dausa: The Early Medieval Township

Well over a thousand years ago, the settlement at Dausa merited enough importance for an inscription to be made during the reign of Mihir Bhoja, or more famously known as Bhoja I (r. 836–92 CE), who is remembered as one of the greatest rulers of the Imperial Pratiharas. This copper plate inscription is known as the Daulatpura Inscription of VS 900 (843 CE), and it concerns land grants by the king.[158]

This confirms that there was a prominent settlement at Dausa, which implies the need for civil as well as defensive infrastructures. Even more important than civil and defensive structures are local sources of water, as throughout most of Rajasthan and Gujarat, water harvesting structures were the essential lifelines of establishing any viable community and township.

The largest of all water sources in Dausa is the ancient baori (stepwell) at the center of the old township located in what is today the shrine of Hazrat Baba Jamaluddin Shah Chisti. The construction style and Hindu motives in the

[158]Atherton, Cynthia Packert, *The Sculpture of Early Medieval Rajasthan*, Brill, Germany, 1997, p. 62; Sharma, Dasharatha, *Rajasthan Through the Ages*, Vol. I, Rajasthan State Archives, Bikaner, 1966, p. 313.

structure clearly indicates that it pre-existed as a public well for the settlement many centuries prior to the founding of the shrine in the late 1600s or early 1700s.

It is believed that the construction of this charming baori may also be attributed to the Badgurjar Rajputs who were contemporary neighbours of the Nikhumbha Rajputs of the Sapadalaksa (Jangaladesa) kingdom.

The Badgurjar and the Nikhumbha Rajputs are attested rulers for much of this area during the time of the Imperial Pratiharas' hegemony as well as after their fall.

In front of the modern main entrance to the Dausa Fort is a maidan-like square, which, as in other medieval Rajasthani townships[159], was used in earlier times as a locale of public gathering and celebrations.

Like many other medieval townships in Rajasthan, the most prominent havelis and temples of Dausa's old township are adjacent to the front portion of the fort. It is evident that a large part of the town's boundary walls did not survive to the present age; the streets of the old township were narrow and haphazard, and it appears that they were constructed as the residential quarters expanded. Evidently, Dausa was an ancient center of Shiavite worship, as demonstrated by the concentration of five Shiva temples known as the 'panch Mahadeo' scattered around the township that has survived till this date. These are:

- Sahajnath Mahadeva temple, located on the Lalsot road, south Dausa.

[159]For an expansion on the description of medieval Rajasthani townships, see Appendix IV.

- Bajanath Mahadeva temple, located on the lower level within Dausa Fort.
- Somthath Mahadeva temple, located on the eastern side on the Jaipur—Bharatpur highway.
- Gupteshwar Mahadeva temple, located in south-west Dausa, near the government girl's college.
- Neelkanth Mahadeva temple, located at the pinnacle of the Dausa Fort hill.

It is no wonder that this hill on which the fort is located is also known locally as Devnagri or 'abode of the Devas'.

How the Fort of Dausa Came into Kachwaha Possession

By the mid-eleventh century, the mighty empire of the Pratiharas had declined and their former feudatories vied for power. The most powerful rulers of central and eastern Rajasthan were certainly the Shakambari branch of the Chauhans, who were the founders of Ajaymeru (Ajmer), as well as the rulers of Delhi.[160]

With regards to Dausa, in particular, it appears that the Chauhans ruled this area in alliance with the Badgurjar Rajputs[161] who were established at Deoti (in Rajgarh tehsil of Alwar district), which was their primary gaddi (seat of power) for many centuries. It is likely that during the early medieval

[160]Hooja, Rima, *A History of Rajasthan*, Rupa & Co., New Delhi, 2006, p. 260.

[161]To this date, their descendants are still to be found in the districts of Dausa, Alwar, Jaipur as well as Bharatpur. For additional information on the Badgurjar Rajputs, please see Appendix VI.

period, the Badgurjars fought under the banner of the Imperial Pratiharas, alongside the Chauhans, Kachaphaghatas and Chandelas, but as explored in Chapter 3, each clan later on became independent chieftains. By the early eleventh to the mid-twelfth centuries, half of the township was said to be in the possession of Badgurjars and the other half under a Chauhan raja (some sources says it was the possession of Ralansi, the Chauhan raja of Lalsot, while other sources say that he was the Chauhan raja of Pachbara-Moran).[162] This situation may have been the result of a military alliance between the Badgurjars and the ruling Chauhans of the area. The Badgurjars were also allied with the Meenas of Dhundhar, who are said to have appealed to the Raja of Deoti during perilous times. However, the brokered peace between the Chauhans and the Badgurjars was, however, a fragile one, and with the entry of a new player on to the scene, the scenario changed irreversibly.

Dulha Rai, the prince who hailed from Gopaksetra on the other side of the Chambal River is said to have gained parts of Dausa as dowry on his marriage with a Chauhan princess, Sojan Kumari, as elaborated in Chapter 5. The Chauhan–Kachwaha alliance resulted in the fort being wrested from the possession of the Badgurjar Rajputs.

Thus, the conquest of Dausa could be seen as the most substantial act in the career of the Kachaphaghata progenitor of the Dhundhar Raj. Through determined effort and dedication, he was able to expand away from his ancestral domain in

[162]Singh Dunlod, Harnath, *Geneological Table of the Kachhawahas*, Navneet Art Printers, Jaipur, p. 10.

Gopaksetra and carve out a principality for himself at Dausa in the Aravalli Hills of north-eastern Rajasthan. With Dausa Fort and district now firmly in Kachwaha procession, the expansionist policy was continued by his immediate successor Kakildeva and his descendants.[163]

Dausa's Role in cementing Kachwaha—Mughal Alliance

The time when Amber was established as the capital of Dhundhar Raj coincided with the sultanate reign in Delhi in the east, when Prithviraj III (popularly known as Prithviraj Chauhan) lost control of the garden city of Indraprasartha to Muhammad Ghori. After the demise of Rana Sanga, the Rajput confederation was broken off, and unity among the major chieftains of Rajputana was lost for many centuries.[164] In this chaotic and tumultuous age, the kingdom of Dhundhar found itself sandwiched between its larger aggressive neighbour within Rajputana (the great Maharaja Maldeo of Marwar snatched away four districts from the Dhundhar Raj) and the rise of Sher Shah Suri. Nonetheless, throughout this period, Dausa stood its ground and was always held firm by the rulers of Amber. The fort continuously retained its local administrative role and was garrisoned by trusted Kachwaha clansmen. This was very much the case at the time of Akbar's

[163]A list of the jagirdars of Dausa under the Jaipur State has been provided in Appendix VII.

[164]It wasn't until the time of the Rajput rebellion against Aurangzeb that there was again unity among the rulers of Mewar, Marwar and Dhundhar, who united to fight against the central Mughal authority.

pivotal visit in 1562 while on a pilgrimage to Ajmer. It must be remembered that this was the time before the alliance between the Kachwahas and the Mughals had been solidified, and the dust of political stability in north India had yet to settle. Sher Shah's less-abled successor, Islam Shah, had just died in 1554, and Akbar, a mere boy of 13, was enthroned in 1556. Thus, it was a precarious time for the rulers of Amber, wary of the aggression of its neighbours, such as Marwar to the northwest, as well as the ambitions of various Mughal warlords.

The fort of Dausa was, at that time, under the command of Rupsi Bairgi, the younger son of Raja Prithviraj of Amber and his Gaud queen Sohag Devi.[165] He was, therefore, a close clansmen of Amber's ruler Bharmal (grandfather of the renowned Mirza Raja Man Singh I of Amber). While Akbar was camping in the territory of Dausa, he was met by Jaimal, who was sent ahead by his father Rupsi, thakur (baron) of Dausa, to survey and report on the disposition of the young Mughal sovereign. This initial meeting must have been a pleasant one, for Jaimal was later granted the Fatehpur pargana as jagir by Akbar.[166]Additionally, he informed his father of Akbar's reasonable and forthright character, thus, Rupsi and other local leaders came forward to meet with the young emperor. An interesting episode is recorded here that bears testimony to Akbar's character. According to Sarkar (based on the accounts of the *Akbarnama*), Akbar had noticed that while passing through the territory of local rulers, that

[165]Sarkar, Jadunath, *A History of Jaipur c. 1503–1938*, Raghubir Sinh (ed.), Orient Longman, 1984, p. 43.
[166]Ibid.

inhabitants of those land had all but fled away due to memory of the trepidation from the times of earlier Muslim rulers. A day after Akbar met with Jaimal and Rupsi, it was reported to him that an imperial cheetah-keeper had robbed a villager of his shoes. By Akbar's orders, the feet of the cheetah-keeper was cut off and news of this incident spread throughout the region, after which villagers no longer ran away upon the passing of Akbar's camp.[167] Having just forged a good rapport with the Rajputs, it seems evident that this minor act of pilferage by his underling must have touched Akbar's raw nerve, as it reflected badly on himself and the fledging reputation he was trying to establish. Through his forthright punishment of the wrongdoer, the young Akbar had proven himself to be a just ruler in the eyes of the Kachwaha nobles as well as the local inhabitants, who spread the word of the emperor's act of justice done against his own retinue.

Mirza Raja Jai Singh I and Dausa

Another lesser-known fact about the fort of Dausa is that it served as the shelter for the man who would go on to become one of the greatest Kachwaha commanders in the Mughal Empire, following the traditions of the august Man Singh I of Amber (progenitor of the Rajawats). Indeed, Dausa garh was the chosen site which Sisodia Rani Damiyanti (daughter of Saha, the brother of Rana Sagar and a granddaughter of Maharana Udai Singh of Mewar), chief rani of Maha Singh (son of Raja Man Singh's eldest son, Jagat Singh) chose as

[167]Ibid.

a secure shelter for her infant son.[168] Born on 16 July 1611, Jai Singh, aged two, was sent away to Dausa to protect him from the intrigues and potentially deadly rivalry at Amber. It was here at Dausa that the future Mirza Raja Jai Singh I spent his childhood and was educated until the age of nine. Although we do not know the names of his tutors, he must have enjoyed a distinguished education and upbringing during his days spent in Dausa, for he grew up to became among the greatest generals and diplomats of the Mughal Empire throughout the reigns of Shahjahan and Aurangzeb. In the words of Jadunath Sarkar:

> At the end of the year 1657, came the most momentous revolution in the Delhi monarchy, which at once called up Jai Singh to the foremost place among the officers of the state and made him play a decisive part in shaping the history of the house of Timur. He defeated Shuja, captured Dara, neutralized Jaswant and conquered the invincible Shivaji.[169]

It was nearly two years after he left Dausa that Jai Singh I acceded to the gaddi of Amber with the blessings of Jahangir at the end of 1621.

It must be repeated that in an age when the borders of a kingdom grew and receded with the fortunes of the state's ruler, the pargana of Dausa was always held by the rulers of Amber, and, unlike other districts, never slipped out of their hands. In fact, when Sawai Jai Singh II inherited the

---

[168]Ibid. 93.

[169]Ibid. 105.

gaddi of Amber, the fortune of the state had sunk so much during the reign of his father Raja Bishan Singh that only three parganas, namely Amber, Dausa and Baswa, were the 'watan jagir' of the ruler of Amber. Nonetheless, these three parganas were sufficient when coupled with the genius of Sawai Jai Singh II, that the total area of Dhundhar state grew from a mere 3,000 square miles to over 20,000 square miles by the end of his reign.[170]

The Battle of Tunga

The reign of Sawai Pratap Singh (r. 1778–1803) was a turbulent period in north Indian history, as the Mughal Empire was in terminal decline. During his reign, the district of Dausa, being situated to Jaipur's east, inevitably witnessed hosts of armies attempting to march towards the famed city of Jaipur. On 28 April 1787, the district was the ground for the battle of Tunga, which was a face-off between the Jaipur army against the Marathas led by the famed Mahadji (Madhorao) Scindia, who was at that time acting out his role as 'Vakil-i-Mutlaq' of the waning Mughal Empire. During this period, there was thankfully a close alliance between the Maharaja of Jaipur and the Maharaja Bijay Singh of Jodhpur, thus the Jaipur army was joined by 5,000 Rathore cavalry as well as 5,000 mercenary Naga gosains (fighting monks/musketeers).

The battle took place on the plain between Tunga and Bidakha, around 3 kilometres from the village of Lalsot.[171]

[170]Ibid.

[171]This battle is also known in the annals of Rajasthani history as the battle of Lalsot.

The headquarters of Sawai Pratap Singh during this battle was the fort of Madhogarh, which offers an expansive view of the whole of the terrain, including the battleground of Lalsot. This battle is rightfully remembered as a victory of the combined Rajput and (defected) Mughal forces (under the command of Muhammad Beg Hamadani) and could be described as the low point in the illustrious career of Mahadji Scindia.

According to Gopal Narayan Bahura, the battle of Tunga was a huge victory for Pratap Singh. He further notes:

> Scindia, the 'Vakil-i-mutlaq' of the emperor with his French generals was put to flight. Though Nawab Hamdani and some brave Rajputs lost their lives yet the prestige of Sawai Pratap singh was raised and songs were sung in his praise as `Victor of the Tunga battle'. He was only twenty years old at that time....[172]

The Battle of Patan

Three years later, the army of Mahadji Scindia and his French commander Colonel Benoît de Boigne, returned with a modernized force and another battle was fought at Patan, north-west of Viratnagar and just north of Shahpura. On one side was the coalition of Jaipur, its Rathore allies and Mughal mercenaries led by the notorious Narnaul Mirza Ismail Beg, with its artillery under the command of Abdul Matlab Khan.

[172]Bahura, G.N., *Pratapa Prakasa: Life in the Jaipur Court In the Late 18th Century*, Maharaja Sawai Man Singh II Museum, City Palace, Jaipur, 1983, p. 8.

On the other side was the combined (but disunited) regiments of Scindia and Holkars under the generalship of Gopal Bhau along with battalions of the famous French commander de Boigne. It was, interestingly, a trench warfare, which started from 20 May with intermittent fighting on both sides and only concluded with the main battle on 20 June 1790. A description of the heat of the battle is given in the words of none other than Jadunath Sarkar:

> During the confusion of this life and death struggle in the centre, Ismail Beg with his Mughalia horse and sepoy battalions had moved up against the Maratha left wing (under Ambaji) and at first carried everything before him. But De Boigne immediately after worsting the Rathor horse, turned his guns upon Ismail and raked him with a flank fire (from Abdul Matlab's captured guns, now served by his own artillery men). The Persian's artillery was silenced; his followers fell fast or fled before a murderous fire to which he could not reply; and at last he admitted the inevitable, flung away his blood-stained sword and galloped back to his tent in hopeless defeat. His commandants Abdul Matlab and Alaya Beg sought their own safety, abandoning their sepoys to their fate.[173]

This was the first time that the cavalry of Rajputana were introduced to the cold steely embrace of the bayonet from de Boinge's battalion. Its chilling effectiveness combined with de Boinge's martial sharpness in utilizing the captured

[173]Sarkar, Jadunath, *A History of Jaipur c. 1503–1938*, Raghubir Sinh (ed.), Orient Longman, 1984, p. 294.

Jaipur guns on its allied Mughlai battalions vitally led to his victory.

However, Mahadji Scindia was not able to follow up this triumph with an invasion of Jaipur, which was still heavily defended. Instead, he opted to utilize his forces for his reconquest of Ajmer and invasion of Marwar. This time, it was Jaipur's turn to send a detachment of 4,000 men to join and assist the Marwar army.[174]

In 1792, the forces of Holkar led by Tukoji Holkar and his Pindaris from their base in Manpur raided Dhundhar and encamped in Dausa. An agreement was worked upon by Rodoji Khawas, the emissary of Sawai Pratap Singh, and the Maratha Tukoji Holkar, in which the pargana of Rampur was ceded to the Holkars (August 1791). However, the fact that Rodoji Khawas was dismissed from his ministerial post and thrown into prison upon his return to Jaipur, is evidence of the maharaja's displeasure about the outcome.[175] It was also during this period that Tonk was severed from Dhundhar, eventually becoming the domain of the nawabs of Tonk. Nonetheless, throughout this turbulent period, the ancient fortress of Dausa stood its ground and was never captured by enemy forces.

On January 1792, Sawai Pratap Singh himself met with and reached an agreement with Tukoji Holkar at Dausa. It was agreed upon that Holkar[176] would assist the maharaja

[174]Ibid. 300.

[175]Rodoji Khawas was able to get himself out of prison after paying a fine of seven lakhs.

[176]In return for his service rendered, Holkar was to receive half of these recovered territories.

in recovering lost territories from the rebellious Rao Raja of Macheri (Alwar).[177]

Dausa During the Great Mutiny

The last military engagement in the vicinity of Dausa took place during the reign of Sawai Ram Singh II, during the great Revolt of 1857. Although little known, it is significant, as it was the last battle fought by Ramachandra Panduranga, better known as Tatya Tope, the abled Maratha commander who actively fought against British forces since May 1857. During the course of the great Mutiny, he was able to defeat the British several times, even capturing the fort of Gwailor, forcing the Scindia maharaja to flee to Agra, leaving behind his harem, all of whom were courteously treated[178] by the rebels, although the treasury was looted. Nonetheless, it was here at Dausa that what was left of Tatya Tope's forces were joined by his (then) allies Maan Singh (of Narwar) and Firoz Shah of Rohilkhand. The motley force of about 2,000 men were met by the better-equipped British forces on 14 January 1859. According to Jaiwant Paul:

> It seemed impossible for Tatya Tope and his men to escape, but escape they did. A British force bore down on them at Dausa, near Jaipur on 14th January 1859. The rebels lost many of their men, but the rest of their leaders got away. They were surprised again at Sikar,

[177]Hooja, Rima, *A History of Rajasthan*, Rupa & Co., New Delhi, 2006, p. 682.
[178]They were escorted to the safety of the ancient fortress of Narwar.

north of Jaipur on 21 January, and after a skirmish once again they disappeared.[179]

From then on, the gallant Tatya Tope would only fight on with guerilla tactics, while continuing to evade the British until his capture and execution on 18 April 1859. For the British, this marked the official and final ending of the Mutiny, as the last and one of the most-able rebels (or freedom fighter) was dead.

Post-Independence Period

Of importance to the modern period in Indian history is the fact that Dausa district is the birthplace of prominent freedom fighters who struggled for India's independence, such as the late Shri Tikaram Paliwal and Shri Ram Karan Joshi. After the inception of the Indian Union, these two personalities gained prominent roles in Rajasthan's early political process. Shri Tikaram Paliwal became the first elected chief minister of Rajasthan in 1952. Shri Ram Karan Joshi, on the other hand, was the one who submitted the first Panchayati Raj Bill in the Vidhan Sabha in 1952, and became the first Panchayati Raj minister of Rajasthan. Thus, the republican model of governance returned to the land of Matsyadesha, as it did periodically in the land since ancient times.

As for the fort of Dausa, due to the fact that it was a property of the Jaipur princely state and not a personal property of any jagirdar, following the merger of Jaipur into the Indian Union, the fort passed onto the hands of the Neelkanth Mahadev

---

[179] Paul, E. Jaiwant, *The Greased Cartridge: The Heroes and Villians of 1857–1858*, Roli Books, 2011.

Temple Trust, which is its custodian till date.

Today, the central ground of the fort where ancient warriors once camped and rode off into battle serves as a different sort of battleground, a football stadium and sports facility, which is very popular with the local youths.

This is by no means a complete history of Dausa, as there are many more historic sites and ruins with fascinating history to be discovered in the vicinity. However, it is my hope that this chapter would at least bring to light some hitherto little-known facts about this important district of the former Dhundhar Raj.

SIX

THE FORT AND SIGNIFICANT SITES OF DAUSA

Dausa Fort

Now we turn our attention to the centrifugal structure of Dausa's township, the garh or fort of Dausa. Rajput forts, which not only acted as the residence of the rulers but also as administrative centre and military base, are often designed in an asymmetrical manner, best utilizing the elevation of the landscape to the advantage of the defenders. Tillotson states that the irregularity of the majority of Rajput forts is largely due to the spasmodic growth of the palace and requirements of each ruler over long periods.[180]

[180]Tillotson, Giles, *The Rajput Palaces: The Development of an Architectural Style, 1450–1750,* Oxford University Press, Delhi, 1999, pp. 35–36.

A.C.L. Carlyle, an Archaeological Survey of India officer, who did a survey of the Dausa region in 1871–72 during the time of Sawai Ram Singh II, provides an impressive description of the hill that makes up the nucleus of Dausa Fort:

> This hill is somewhat narrow, and perfectly precipitous or almost perpendicular, or on its northern face. The eastern face is also steep, but there is a slope on its western face. The southern side of the hill, however, extends out for some distance, sending forth broken, rocky spurs, enclosing a deep, crater shaped hollow. Indeed, it has every appearance of being the remains of the crater of an ancient extinct volcano.[181]

In the eyes of ancient rulers, the 'crater' which made up the hill of Dausa Fort would have been easily recognized as a natural spot meriting the construction of a *guha-durga* (fort built in a valley surrounded by hills that provides natural defence) type of stronghold. It also incorporates characteristics of the *giri-parshva-durga* (fort built down the slopes of a hill), as any individual castle could and usually does combine different types of defensive characteristics based on the merits of its natural location and the ingenuity of the rulers and his architects.[182] In the case of Dausa Fort, being situated 1,643 metres above sea level, the crescent-shaped hill surrounding a valleyed crater acted as a natural defensive

---

[181]Carlyle, A.C.L., *Report of a Town in Eastern Rajputana in 1871-72*, Indological Book House, Varanasi, 1966, p. 104.

[182]For further description on the types of hill/mountain strongholds mentioned in old shastras, please see Appendix V.

structure, thus, only the frontal fortification needed to be constructed in order to establish a stronghold.

Carlyle also recorded to have found some megalithic stone circles in the vicinity of the fort, which he describes in so many words:

> On the gently sloping ground to the north of the foot of the hill, I discovered the remains of four stone circles, which I believe to have probably been the work of aborigines, during the archaic or pre-historic period.
>
> The most westerly placed of these circles was about 24 feet in diameter. Eleven of its stones were in position, and three more stones had been rolled away out of place from the circle, on its south side. Of the eleven stones in position, six were on the northern curve of the circle, and three on its southern curve; and here were two stones standing together in the centre of the circle.[183]

It is interesting to note that Carlyle compared the monoliths of pre-historic Dausa with the Druidical standing stones found in the British Isles. He also speculated Dausa may 'have been one of the most anciently fortified sites in Rajputana'. Today, it is regrettable to report, that the stone circles of Dausa no longer exist, equally forgotten is the mystery of its origins.

The frontal fortification of Dausa Fort is an outer wall interspersed with towers (*attakala*) that are lesser in height than the inner walls (thus allowing double amount of projectiles to be showered onto potential attackers). The

---

[183]Carlyle, A.C.L., *Report of a Town in Eastern Rajputana in 1871-72*, Indological Book House, Varanasi, 1966, pp. 104–105.

inner walls are impressively high ramparts, which forces visitors/invaders to enter into the winding uphill road flanked by curtain walls leading to a carefully designed series of gateways, a typical feature of Hindu defensive architecture. It is regrettable that the walls on the outer side of this fortified road as well as the boundary walls below have not been preserved and have suffered the onslaught of time.

The central ground of Dausa Fort's valleyed enclave is large enough to have served as an arable land, but whether or not this function it ever served we cannot say for certain. Most likely, it served as camping quarters in times of war or emergency, or an encampment ground for the army as well as for fielding troops practising cavalry manoeuvers, among other usages relating to medieval military functions. Remnants of elephant and horse stables are still recognizable in the fort's precincts, although they are crumbling away, a fate shared by much of Rajasthan's historical and architectural heritage over the past 70 years.

The last alteration done at this fort most probably dates to the time of Sawai Jai Singh II, as it was during his reign that widespread refurbishment of pre-existing defensive structures took place throughout the Dhundhar Raj.

As one enters the inner sanctum of the fort, one encounters to the right hand side, an impressive and large baori, which must have been an original feature of the fort and likely predates the capture of the fort by the Kachwahas.

One also notices a number of temples located within the fort, built upon earlier structures—Bajinath Mahadev temple, Shiv Shakti Maha yah mandir and Durga Mandir.

Additionally, there is a mosque known as the Jama Masjid,

which would have accommodated visitors and soldiers from the Mughal period onwards.

In both the Hindu or Muslim strongholds of India, the palace was the principle building inside a fort. According to Kautilya, the palace should be placed towards the north of the city centre and should occupy one-ninth of the whole site, with its front facing either east or north, while other treatises advise that the palace should be built at the center of a fortress. In actuality, the palace was built at the center of a walled city or flat fortress, whereas on a hill or mountain, the palace would naturally sit at the least accessible point. In the case of Dausa garh, the least accessible part of the fort is the summit, where today stands the Neelkanth Mahadev (Shiva) temple, which appears to have been built upon a much earlier structure (it is also the least accessible temple in Dausa, requiring due effort on a sunny day). As the temple is located within a fortified precinct at the highest and most secure part of the castle, it may be reasonable to suspect that it was perhaps this summit that once served as the palatial living quarters of Dausa Fort, while the Shiavite shrine also most likely existed. However, as the palace grew into disuse over the centuries (although the rest of the fort was used for administrative and military purposes), the temple continuously grew until it took over the entire palatial structure, thus resulting in this unusual fortified temple (which somewhat reminds one of the Garh Ganeshji Temple in Jaipur).

At present, no palatial structure remains within the fort, understandably, as it served as the capital of Dhundhar for a very brief period, coupled with the fact that over a thousand years has elapsed since the time of Dulha Rai and his sons.

With reference to antiquities discovered within Dausa Fort, archeologist Rai Bahadur Daya Ram Sahni notes:

> These include a collection of some 40 to 50 fragments of stone images of some of the principal Hindu gods and goddesses, red Karauli stone pilasters adorned with the vase and palmette and other patterns, crocodile mouthed gargoyles, and a large stone linga, whose top alone is a visible above the ground, which originally belonged to a Siva temple which stood on the summit of the hill and whose site is now occupied by a later temple of Nilkantha Mahadeva standing within a small fortified citadel. One or two small guns in the fort bear Nagari inscriptions dated Vikrama samvaat 1849, etc. Another group of finely carved sculptures of about the 12th century A.D. is worshipped in or built into the front wall of a modern temple known as Mataji-ka-mandir. Among these antiquities are a well preserved image of the sun, window lintels etc. A largish mound outside the Mori Darwaza of the fort, which is partly occupied by what is known as Bhaumyaji-ka-mahal, deserves excavation.[184]

Regardless of where the original palatial structure stood, it is imperative to remember that it was from this very stronghold that Dulha Rai launched his attacks on the neighbouring strongholds of the Meenas and the Badgurjars, which eventually resulted in the inception of Dhundhar state, which

[184]Sahni, Daya Ram, *Excavations at Bairat*, Publication Scheme, Jaipur, 1999, pp. 8–9.

was the seat of premier power in Rajputana by the middle of the eighteenth century.

Places of Interest within Dausa Township and District

Shree Surajmal Bhomiya Ji Maharaj Temple

At a short distance overlooking the maidan ground and Dausa Fort lies the Surajmal Bhomiya Ji temple. This is a highly revered place for locals and visitors to Dausa alike, and particularly for the Rajputs, as it commemorates and keeps alive the worship of a Kachwaha prince who fell fighting to defend the land and thus became a Bhomiya ji (Bhomiyas are warriors who heroically fell in battle and are worshiped for their sacrifice and devotion, their deeds are often recorded on 'hero stones' found throughout Rajasthan).

I fondly remember my first visit to Dausa in which I was warmly received by the locals. It was here that a small puja was conducted and our respects paid to Bhomiya ji. A large gathering then took place within the compound of this temple and it was perhaps this memorable experience that inspired me to undertake the writing of this book.

The temple is now under the care of pundit Sunil Kumar Pareek, whose family has been the custodian to this temple for over four generations. Pandit ji fondly recounted the visit of my late uncle H.H. Sawai Bhawani Singh and my grandmother the late Rajmata Gayatri Devi to this temple. Being an ancestral temple, pujas are conducted here particularly on Mondays, the auspicious day for offering prayers to Lord Shiva or family ancestors, whereas large congregations of visitors also come here during Dusshera.

The Mysterious Case of the Baswa Cremation Mound

There is a curious episode in Dausa's history believed by the locals to be related to Rana Sanga of Mewar. This is due to the existence of an old *chabutra* (cremation platform) adjacent to the railway track near the village of Baswa, 15 kilometres north of Banikui railway station, which is said to be associated with Rana Sanga of Mewar. There is a belief among the locals that this chabutra marked the cremation spot of Rana Sanga, the famed warrior king, who died six months after the battle of Khanau (17 March 1527). During the battle of Khanau, the Kachwaha raja of Amber was part of the Rajput confederation that is said to have rallied as much as 200,000 horsemen under a single banner led by Rana Sanga, as Dausa would have been a friendly territory for the Rajput coalition on the march south-westwards towards Hadoti and Mewar. However, the correct date and place of Rana Sanga's death has, according to no other than Sir Jadunath Sarkar, 'been subject to great controversy'.[185] Alas, there is another legend that asserts that Rana Sanga was poisoned and died while on his way to Mandalgarh, where he was cremated on 30 January 1528.[186]

Thus, while it is impossible to validate the story behind the chabutra in Baswa, due to lack of any first- or second-hand material, it is obvious that the person who was cremated here

[185]Sarkar, Jadunath, *A History of Jaipur c. 1503–1938,* Raghubir Sinh (ed.), Orient Longman, 1984, p. 30.

[186]Hooja, Rima, *A History of Rajasthan,* Rupa & Co., 2006, p. 456.

was highly ranked, that it caused the chabutra to be raised and remain intact for many centuries. It is possible that the chabutra is the spot where Rana Sanga met his demise, or else it could have been one of his generals.

Shah Jamaluddin Chisti Dargah

The Shah Jamaluddin Chisti Dargah occupies the space where once stood the ancient baori, which in earlier periods undoubtedly served as the center of the township for many centuries. This shrine is said to have been established in the early eighteenth century. The story of how the dargah came into being goes along the lines that after the passing away of his wife in faraway Arabia, Shah Jamal was told by his peers to pay a visit to the dargah of Shaikh Moinuddin Chisti at Ajmer. Having visited the holy dargah at Ajmer, Shah Jamal experienced an epiphany and was further told by his peers that he should settle down at Dausa. Having first settled down at a place called Ashwari Doongri, he later on came to stay at the ancient baori in the middle of Dausa's township. From this point onwards, the Sufi mystic continuously served the poor and needy in this vicinity; he is also said to have formed a bond of friendship with a Brahmin called Chand Mal. The two friends are remembered to have spread the message of peace, love and communal harmony through the rest of their lives.

It is remembered that Shah Jamal lived until the ripe old age of 80, and that he was visited by both Maharaja Sawai Madho Singh I of Jaipur and the Maharaja of Karauli (which is in very close proximity to Dausa). Both had evidently heard of his fame and came to consult the saint, and both are said to have had their wishes fulfilled as a result of the visit!

Today, the shrine is a symbol of unity and is worshipped by all communities in Dausa, with a particularly large congregation on Wednesday nights. It is now under the administration of a committee officially set up by the Rajasthan Board of Muslim Waqfs.

Purana Khera and Kherapata Hanuman Mandir

Towards the backside of the fort, there is a small settlement known as Purana Khera. According to the local priest, this used to be a vibrant settlement in the distant past, but it was abandoned at some point, and it has only in the past few decades been repopulated by a handful of households. It is also home to the Kherapati Hanuman Mandir.

There is also the murti of a fallen warrior or Bhairoji here, which is now being worshiped. However, due to the fact that Purana Khera was not continuously inhabited, the history of this particular Bhairoji seems to be lost.

The Stepwell and Temple of Abhaneri

The eighth-century stepwell of Abhaneri (also known as the Chand Baori) is, arguably, the most famous baori of Rajasthan. It is said to be constructed as a 'Vijaya Vapi' based on lord Vishvakarma's Vastusastra and the Aprajitapricha.[187] The temple is believed to have been built by Raja Chanda, a Chauhan Rajput ruler of the Nikumbha family, and is, thus, the source of its popular name. The baori boasts of a large

[187]Yadav, Rajendra, *Sculptural Art of Abaneri: A Paradigm*, Jawahar Kala Kendra, Jaipur, 2006, p. 12.

number of sculptures from the Pratihara period preserved in the pavilion, which are worth spending time to study if one is interested in the iconographic art of post-Gupta/ Pratihara period.

The beauty and symmetry of this baori stuns visitors from around the world, as its dramatic size and setting is a sight that delights the imagination. However, one would require a book in its own right to describe the history, architecture and symbolism of this marvel that is well over a thousand years old.

The Chand Baori is separated 70 meters away from the Harshatmata Temple, dated to 800–23 CE. Despite its fairly modern name, the original temple prior to its destruction at an unknown date is believed to have been a fine example of Vaishnavite temple architecture, comparable to the Kumbhasvami Temple of Chittorgarh as well as the eighth-century Harihara Temple of Osian.[188]

The current structure is, in fact, a later reconstruction using the original materials that were scattered all over the area. After the reconstruction, the temple became a shrine for the goddess Durga; however, after the murti of Durga was stolen, an image of the goddess Lakshmi was installed, giving the temple its current name.

Mahendipur Balaji Mandir

Lastly, a historic survey of Dausa would not be complete without mentioning the Mahendipur Balaji mandir, which is the most popularly visited temple of Dausa today. The

[188]Ibid.

fame of this temple is based on the sanctity of Lord Balaji or Hanuman's murti and the healing power believed to be associated with it, which he grants to those suffering from afflictions of various sorts.

This is by no means a complete list of historic sites of interest in Dausa, as there are many more hidden gems and places of historical significance to be discovered by tourists as well as locals throughout eastern Rajasthan. It is my hope that the younger generation would be proud and delighted in the study of the local history of Dausa, which would hopefully lead to further research, exploration as well as conservation of historic sites in this fascinating district of Dausa.

APPENDIX I

MYSTERY OF THE NAGAS

Puranic sources as well as numismatic evidence found from Padmavati all the way up to Mathura suggest that from the first to third century CE, the area was ruled by a dynasty termed by historians as the Nagas of Vidisha, Padmavati, Kantipuri and Mathura. According to Dr. R.K. Sharma, the Nagas 'began its political career sometime towards the close of the second century A.D., and emerging into prominence when the foreign Kushan power was disintegrating, succeeding in driving it out from the Gangetic valley.' However,

> The evidence of the Puranas about the rulers of this dynasty is vague and carries little practical value and it has given rise to sharp differences of opinions amongst scholars. The Vishnu Puarana, for example, discloses the existence of nine (nava) Naga kings who ruled at Padmavati, Kantipuri and Mathura and this account is

> corroborated by the Vayu Purana, which mentions only two houses of the Nagas, once at Padmavati and the other at Mathura. The number of kings at each of the places being stated to be nine and seven respectively. The rulers of the Naga dynasty at Vidisha have also been referred to by the Puranas.[1]

Through the analysis of numismatic evidence found in the local area it is now believed that they were one of the leading powers and ousted the Kushans from the Gangetic plains to Mathura (as Kushan coins were replaced by Naga coins in these vicinities of Mathura, Padmavati to Kantipuri).[2]

Based on the language used on their coinage, it could clearly be seen that the Nagas were a Sanskritized and cultured people, not simple heathens living in the jungle.

After several centuries of rule, we next know that the Nagas of Mathura and Padmavati were defeated by the Guptas. Although the Guptas are known for their policy of allowing local kings to retain their thrones as long as they paid tribute, there is evidence that the Naga kingdom, having submitted, rose in revolt during the reign of Samudragupta, as according to Schmidt:

> Following earlier pattern, Samudragupta forced vassal status upon a dozen different states, apparently as far south as Kanchi. Before he could complete his conquest

[1]Sharma, R.K., 'Ancient History of the Naga Tribe of Central India and their cultural contributions', *Dimension of Human Cultures in Central India*, A.A. Abbasi (ed.), Sarup & Sons, 2001, pp. 143–44.
[2]Ibid. p. 156.

> of the south, however, Samudragupta was forced to return to the north to quell a growing resistance to his overlordship among the Naga rulers in an area known as Aryavarta. Once he had destroyed the resistance of the Naga Kings, Samudragupta conquered the Shakas of Eran, followed by a successful campaign in Bundelkhand.[3]

In reference to the Naga king Ganapati, R.K Sharma had this to say: 'This name has been included in the Allahabad pillar inscription of Samudragupta in the list of Kings whom he violently exterminated, and in view of this statement Ganapati may be regarded as the last of the Naga Kings whose kingdom was annexed to the Gupta empire.'[4]

Although the above statements point out the demise of the major Naga kingdom with its capital at Padmavati, Naga confederacies in western Madhya Pradesh as well as many parts of Rajasthan seem to have continued for many centuries until sometime in the twelfth century. Subsequently, the remaining Naga principalities may have either mutated their name or been assimilated into the rising powers of the area.

An interesting excerpt is given based on a traditional couplet:

> *Parmaran rughaviya Naga gaya Patal*
> *Raha bapda asiya, kinri jhumey chaal*

[3]Schmidt, Karl J., *An Atlas and Survey of South Asian History*, Taylor & Francis, 2015, p. 24.

[4]Sharma, R.K., 'Ancient History of the Naga Tribe of Central India and their cultural contributions', *Dimension of Human Cultures in Central India*, A.A. Abbasi (ed.), Sarup & Sons, 2001, p. 157.

According to Rima Hooja, 'this couplet implies that upon being defeated by the Parmars, the Nagas have gone to rule over Patal (the underworld).'[5]

There have been several interpretations of patal, keeping in mind that the Nagas of southern India were great seafarers, thus the enigma of the Nagas endure.

[5]Hooja, Rima, *A History of Rajasthan*, Rupa & Co., New Delhi, 2006, p. 163.

APPENDIX II

A POSSIBLE EXPLANATION OF HOW THE KACHWAHA NAME CAME ABOUT

The term Kachwaha only gained popular and wide usage after the clan's total reinvigoration spearheaded by Raja Man Singh I, and this view is supported by Rima Hooja:

> Epigraphs like the Balvan Inscription of AD 1288, Chatsu Inscription of AD 1499, Sanganer Inscription of AD 1601, and Rewasa Inscription of AD 1604 refer to the dynasty as 'Kurma'. Apparently the term 'Kachhawa' became more popular from about the late sixteenth century during the reign of Raja Man Singh of Amber. Poets of that period, like Amritraj in his Mancharitra Kavya composed in AD 1585, Narottam in his Mancharitra, and Murari Das in Man Prakash Kavya, have used the term Kurma or

Kurmbha for Raja Man Singh's dynasty.[6]

It must be remembered that after centuries of near terminal decline, the power of the Kachwahas was gradually restored under the efforts of Raja Bharmal in the mid-sixteenth century. This policy was continued by Bhagwan Das and reached its apex during the reign of Raja Man Singh I of Amber. The palace of Amber built by Raja Man Singh I, being a testimony to his power, served as a reminder to people passing through the old trade route of this fact. This led to the clan being almost totally reinvented in all its aspect, including its popular name, as all evidence suggests.

Lastly, there is the important fact that another popular epithet of this clan is Kushwaha, which denotes their claim of Suryavanshi origin. Lord Kush being the second son of the legendary antediluvian dharma king Lord Ram of Ayodhya. Thus, one could perhaps recognize that the presently popular Kachwaha, while originating from the much older Kachaphaghata and Kurmba is, in fact, either a distorted form of Kushwaha or possibly a new name coined by combining the two, as demonstrated below:

Kachapaghata + Kush**waha** = **Kachwaha**

Thus, the name Kachwaha was adopted by the clan from the time of Raja Man Singh I of Amber onwards.

[6]Hooja, Rima, *A History of Rajasthan*, Rupa & Co., New Delhi, 2006, p. 390.

APPENDIX III

THE ASHOKAN EDICTS OF BHABRU-CALCUTTA AND BAIRAT[7]

- BHABRU-CALCUTTA-BAIRAT MINOR ROCK EDICT

Conversion into Pali Roman Transcript:

1. Piyadassi magadho raja samgham abhivadanto aha, appabadhatum ca phasu viharatum ca
2. Vidito evam bhante, yavatako aham Buddhasmim, Dhammasmim, Samghasmim garavo ca pasado ca yo koci bhante.
3. Bhafava Buddhena bhasita sabbe esa subhasita. Evam ca kho bhante amhehi desito.

[7]The contents of this appendix have been sourced from Hultzsch, E., Inscriptions of Asoka. New Edition. In: Corpus Inscriptionum Indicarum vol. I, Clarendon Press, Oxford, 1925, pp. 171-72.

4. Eham sudhammo, ciratthitiko hohissati iti. Arahami aham, tam vattabbo imani bhante dhammapariyayani vinayasamukaso.
5. Arouava,samo, anagatabhayani, munigatha moneyyasuttani, Upatissapanham, evam ca Rathulavado.
6. Musavado adhikicco, Bhagava Buddhena bhasito, etani bhante dhammapariyayani icchami
7. Kimci, bahuni bhikhavo ca bhikhumyo abhikkhanam ca suneyyum ca upadhareyyum ca.
8. Evam evam upasaka ca upasika ca. Etaya bhante idam likheyyami, abhippetam mama janantu iti.

1. Desito = expounded, shown, taught
2. Araha = worthy of, deserving, entitled to
3. Pasino = panh = question
4. Adhikicca = Adhi (a prefix)- kicca (katabbam)= well understood

Translation:

1. The beloved of God, king of Magadh conveys his regards to Samgha and wishes less obstacles and comforts at Vihara.
2. It is known to you oh brethren, as far as I am concerned (inclined), my respect and devotion (goes) to Buddha, Dhamma and Samgha, Whatever, oh brethren.
3. Lord Buddha had said is all well said. This is what I have (instructed) expounded. This good law will last for long.

4. I say that which deserves to say. These, oh reverend ones, are disquisitions of Dhamma (and praise) of Vinaya.
5. Ariya Vansa, dangers that may occur in future, verses of monks, suttas of monks, and a Question of Upatissa, similarly Rahula-vada.
6. Musavada have been well understood. All these have been said by Lord Buddha, oh, reverend ones, I desire them, as a disquisition on Bhamma.
7. Some, and many monks and nuns should hear them and follow them, every moment.
8. Similarly, this should be applied to lay devotees and female lay devotees too. For this purpose, oh reverend ones, I am inscribing (writing); know the motive behind this (writings).

- (CALCUTTA) THE BAIRAT MINOR ROCK EDICT

Roman Transcript:

1. Devanam piye aha sati...
2. Vasani ya hakam upasake no chu badham...
3. Am mamaya samghe upayati badh ca...
4. Jambudipasi amisa no devehi...mi.. kamasa esa....le
5. No hi ese mahatamena cakiye...kamaminena
6. Vipule pi svage cakye aladhetave...ka ca udala palakamatu ti
7. Anta pi ca janamtu cilathita... lam pi vadhisati...
8. Diyamdhiyam vadhisati....
   (Place: Rajasthan)

Pali Roman Transcript:

1. Devanamppiya aha sati...
2. Vassani yada aham upasako, na balham ca..
3. Atha maya samgham upasito, balham co...
4. Jambudipasmim amissa na devehi...mi... parakkamassa eso phalam
5. Na hi eso mahanto eva sakkoti... parakkamena
6. Vipulam api saggam sakkoti, aradhetum...(khudd) ko ca ularo ca parakkamantu, iti
7. Anta api ca janeyyum, cirahitiko... (vipu)lam api vaddhissati....
8. Patidinam vaddhissati...

Translation:

1. Thus said the beloved God.
2. I have been a lay devotee for.... Years but no exceeding....
3. But when I personally (served) Samgha then exceeding....
4. In Hambudipa, Godly ones were not mixing with... this is a fruit of exertion.
5. Not that only higher one can do (possible).... With exertion....
6. Much (fruit can be obtained), possible to obtain heaven, accomplished... lower ones and higher ones, by exerting.
7. Others living on borders should also know about it, it will last a long time and increase exceedingly...
8. Day by day it will grow (increase)...

APPENDIX IV

DESCRIPTION OF TYPICAL TOWNSHIPS IN RAJASTHAN

According to Aniruddha Ray:

> The towns of Rajasthan grew mainly around the forts. Many of these had commercial connections. In course of time these towns created defensive works by surrounding itself with walls although the fort with its own wall remained separate from the city. The king was often of the same caste as those of the principal inhabitants of the city. But one could see the physical separation from them, except perhaps in time of crisis. The king had his palace within the fort while some of the leading nobles too had their houses inside the fort. Outside the fort the market dominated with its central location, from where generally two roads lead to the gates of the city. But one does not see any regular pattern within the

> central place or in its periphery. The lanes shoot out in different directions from the principal street. Apart from getting revenue from the villages, the towns used to get surplus products of the villages...
>
> Two big streets met at the centre of the city and then extended towards the gates after being divided. Smaller lanes came out of the big street and meandered to various places. The city was divided into different mahallas, some of which were square and some octagonal. There are different types of temples and houses in the city.[8]

Ray also accurately describes how it was typical in medieval Rajasthani townships for Brahmins and Thakurs to reside in separate mohallas, while other communities lived on the edge of the cities or just outside (often in the southern or western side of the township).

[8] Ray, Aniruddha, *Towns and cities of Medieval India*, Manohar, New Delhi, 2015, pp. 53–54.

APPENDIX V

TYPES OF HILL/MOUNTAIN STRONGHOLDS MENTIONED IN ANCIENT SHASTRAS

According to Konstantin S. Nossov[9], there are three types of fortifications:

Prantara-durga: A fortress built on the summit (usually flat) of a hill or a mountain. This was the most common type in the middle ages and the best examples are the castles of Gwalior, Chittor and Ranthambore.

Giri-parshva-durga: Both major civilian structures and fortifications extend down the slope of a hill or mountain, though the summit is certainly included into the defense system too.

[9]Nossov, Konstantin S., *Indian Castles 1206–1526*, Osprey, 2006, pp. 8–9.

Guha-durga: The living quarters are situated in a valley surrounded by high, impassable hills. The hills house a chain of outposts and signal towers connected by extensive defensive walls.

APPENDIX VI

ADDITIONAL INFORMATION ON BADGURJAR RAJPUTS

Accodring to Rima Hooja, 'Inscriptions found at Macheri (known as the Macheri inscriptions), dating to VS 1426 and 1439 indicate that Rajgarh, Macheri and Deoti (Devati) were among the possessions of the Badguars, and were among the small independent chiefships of the time that had successfully withstood the Delhi Sultanate.'[10]

Additionally, the Badgurjars are said to claim descent from Lava, the eldest son of Lord Rama. A.H. Bingley notes, 'The Aligarh branch trace their descent from a Surajbans Raja called Rajdeo who built the fort of Rajor in Jeypore (Jaipur). His great grandson married a daughter of Prithviraj, the Chauhan Raja of Delhi and the emigration of the Bargujars

[10]Hooja, Rima, *A History of Rajasthan*, Rupa & Co., New Delhi, 2006, pp. 410–11.

dates from the time of their son Partab Singh, who was sent by his grandfather to conquer Kumaun.'[11]

[11]Bingley, A.H., *Handbook on Rajputs*, Asian Educational Services, New Delhi, 1986, p. 45.

APPENDIX VII

A list of *thikhanas* (jagirs) of Jaipur State in Dausa distict, followed by the current head of the family, number of villages and the number of cavalry men they contributed to the Jaipur State:

Dhula
Rawal Rahuveer Singhji of Dhula and Bhandarej
45 villages

Khawa
Late Rao Vishve Singh
84 horses

Aluda
Thakur Chander Pal Singh
52 horses

Lawana
Raj Sahib Arvind Kumar Singh

Baniyana
Thakur Shiv Kalyan Singh
45 horses

Gugolan
Thakur Kuber Singh
14 villages and 7 horses

Bada goan
Thakur Madan Singh
5 horses

Birvada (Sikarai)
Thakur Devi Singh
21 horses

Lotwada
Thakur Giriraj Singh (current President of the Rajput Sabha)
12 horses

Beju Pada
Thakur Kushal Singh Lalyanot

Khatva
Thakur Behru Singh
12 horses

Deo Rajvi (Lalsot)
Thakur Devi Singh
84 horses

Madhogarth
Thakur Shiv Pratap Singh Bhatti

Nangal Rajawatan
Thakur Bhoor Singhji
5 horses

Nangal Pyariwas
Thakur Prahlad Singh
5 horses

Nandera (Bandi kui)
Thakur Bhanwar Singh
12 horses

Jeerota
Thakur Suganpal Singh
5 horses

Etayada
Thakur Babu Singh
1 horse

Hamawas (Ramgarh Pachwara)
Thakur Gopal Singh
3 villages and 1 horse

Chavandeda
Thakur Mandan Singh
5 horses

Additionally:

> It was in 1646 AD that Amar Singh, an ancestor of the line, drove out Himmata Mina from Dhula and occupied the place. Dalel Singh reported to have been granted a patta with one and a quarter lakh of rupees by Sawai Jai Singh II at Mathura. He constructed the fort at Dhula in 1757 AD He was killed in the battle of Maonda along with his sons and grandson. Other Rajawats who died with their leaders were Nawal Singh of Lasadya, Dulah Singh of Chavandeda, Simbhu Singh of Rasalpura and Sanwal Singh of Mangalwada.
>
> Raghnath Singh of Dhula displayed conspicuous gallantry at Basawa and repulsed all attacks. He also fought bravely at Bhandarej. Maharaja Pratap Singh honoured him for his success. Rawat Ranjit Singh constructed a fort named Ranjitgarth at Dhula.[12]

[12]Bakshi, S.R., and S.K. Sharma, *Nobility, Society and Administration of Rajputs*, Deep & Deep Publications, New Delhi, 2000, p. 18.

BIBLIOGRAPHY

Abbasi, A.A., *Dimensions of Human Cultures in Central India*, Sarup & Sons, New Delhi, 2001.

Ali, Ahmed, *Kachchhapaghata Art and Architecture*, Publication Scheme, Jaipur, 2005.

Ali, Daud, *Courtly Culture and Political Life in Early Medieval India*, Cambridge University Press, 2004.

Atherton, Cynthia Packert, *The Sculpture of Early Medieval Rajasthan*, Brill, Germany, 1997.

Avari, Burjor, *India: The Ancient Past: A History of the Indian Sub-continent from c.7000 BC to AD 1200*, Routledge, 2007.

Bagchi, Jhunu, *The History and Culture of the Pālas of Bengal and Bihar, Cir. 750 AD-cir. 1200 AD,* Abhinav Publications, New Delhi, 1993.

Bahura, G.N., *Pratapa Prakasa: Life in the Jaipur Court In the Late 18th Century*, Maharaja Sawai Man Singh II Museum, City Palace, Jaipur, 1983.

Bakshi, S.R., and S.K. Sharma, *Nobility, Society and Administration of Rajputs*, Deep & Deep Publications, New Delhi, 2000.

Barton, William, *The Princes of India*, Nisbet & Co., 1934.

Basham, A.L., *The Wonder That was India*, Grove Press, New York, 1954.

Bharucha, Rustom, *Rajasthan: An Oral History: Conversations with Komal Kothari*, Penguin Books, New Delhi, 2003.

Bhatnagar, V.S., *Life and Times of Sawai Jai Singh 1688–1743*, Impex India, Delhi, 1974.

Bingley, A.H., *Handbook on Rajputs*, Asian Educational Services, New Delhi, 1986.

Carlyle, A.C.L., *Report of a Town in Eastern Rajputana in 1871-72*, Indological Book House, Varanasi, 1966.

Chandra, Satish, *History of Medieval India 800–1700*, Orient Blackswan, 2007.

Chattopadhya, B.D., *The Making of Early Medieval India*, Oxford University Press, New Delhi, 2012.

Cunningham, A., *Archaeological Survey of India Report*, 2 Vols, 1871.

Elliot, Henry M., *The History of India as Told by its Own Historians: The Muhammadan Period*, volume 1, Elibron Classics, London, 2006.

Garde, M.B., *Archaeology in Gwalior*, Department of Archaeology, Gwalior State, 1924.

Goetz, Hermann, 'The Historical Background of the Great Temples of Khajuraho', *Arts Asiatiques*, vol. 5, no. 1 (1958).

Henige, David, *Princely States of India: A Guide to Chronology and Rulers*, Orchid Press, Bangkok, 2004.

Hooja, Rima, *A History of Rajasthan*, Rupa & Co., New Delhi, 2006.

Hultzsch, E., *Inscriptions of Asoka*. New Edition. In: Corpus Inscriptionum Indicarum vol. I, Clarendon Press, Oxford, 1925.

Jain, K.C., *Malwa Through The Ages,* Motilal Banarasidass, New Delhi, 1972.

Kolff, D.H.A., *Naukar Rajput and Sepoy: The Ethnohistory of the Military Labour Market in Hindustan, 1450–1850,* Cambridge University Press, 2002.

Majumdar, R.C. (ed.), *The Age of Imperial Kanauj,* Bharatiya Vidya Bhavan, Bombay, 1955.

Mitra, Sisir Kumar, *The Early Rulers of Khajuraho,* Motilal Banarsidass, Delhi, 1977.

Monserrate, Antonio, *The Commentary of Father Monserrate S.J., on His Journey to the Court of Akbar,* translated by J.S. Hoyland, annotated by S. N. Banerjee, Asian Educational Services, New Delhi, 1922.

Muhammad Nazim, *The Life and Times of Sultan Mahmud of Ghazna,* Cambridge University Press, 2014.

Nath, Aman, *Jaipur: The Last Destination,* India Book House, 1996.

Nossov, Konstantin S., *Indian Castles 1206–1526*, Osprey, 2006.

Paul, E. Jaiwant, *The Greased Cartridge: The Heroes and Villians of 1857–1858*, Roli Books, 2011.

Ratnawat, Shyam Singh (ed.), *Kachhawan Ri Vanshavali: A Genealogical Account of the Kacchawa Nobility*, Centre for Rajasthan Studies, University of Jaipur, Jaipur, 1981.

Ray, Aniruddha, *Towns and cities of medieval India*, Manohar, New Delhi, 2015.

Ray, H.C., *The Dynastic History of Northern India: Early Medieval Period*, 2 vols, Munshiram Manoharlal, New Delhi, 1973.

Sahni, Daya Ram, Rai Bahadur, *Excavations at Bairat*, Publication Scheme, Jaipur, 1999.

Sarkar, Jadunath, *A History of Jaipur c. 1503–1938*, Raghubir Sinh (ed.), Orient Longman, 1984.

Schmidt, Karl J., *An Atlas and Survey of South Asian History*, Taylor & Francis, 2015.

Scindia, B.R.B., *History of the Fortress of Gwalior*, Bombay, 1892.

Sharma, Dasharatha, *Early Chauhān Dynasties: A Study of Chauhān Political History, Chauhān Political Institution, and Life in the Chauhān Dominions, from 800 to 1316 A.D.*, Motilal Banarsidass Publishers, Delhi, 1975.

Sharma, Dasharatha, *Rajasthan Through the Ages*, Vol. 1, Rajasthan State Archives, Bikaner, 1966.

Sharma, R.K., 'Ancient History of the Naga Tribe of Central India and their cultural contributions', *Dimension of Human Cultures in central India*, A.A. Abbasi (ed.), Sarup & Sons, 2001.

Sharma, Tej Ram, *A Political History of the Imperial Guptas: From Gupta to Skandagupta*, Concept Publishing Company, Delhi, 1989.

Singh, Dhananajaya, *The House of Marwar: The Story of Jodhpur*, Roli Books, New Delhi, 1994.

Singh Dunlod, Harnath, *Geneological Table of the Kachhawahas*, Navneet Art Printers, Jaipur.

Singh, Upinder, *History of Ancient and Early India: From the Stone Age to the 12th Century*, Pearson Education, 2008.

Tillotson, Giles, *The Rajput Palaces: The Development of an Architectural Style, 1450–1750*, Oxford University Press, 1999.

Tod, James, *Annals and Antiquities of Rajasthan Or the Central and Western Rajput States of India*, volumes I and II, Routledge & Kegan Paul, 1972.

Tod, James, *Annals and Antiquities of Rajast'han, or, The Central and Western Rajpoot States of India*, Vol 2, Smith, Elder and Co, Cornhill, Calkin and Budd, Fall Mall, 1832.

Wadley, Susan Snow, *Raja Nal and the Goddess: The North Indian Epic Dhola in Performance*, Indiana University Press, 2004.

Willis, Michael D., 'An Introduction to the Historical Geography of Gopaksetra, Dasarna and Jejakadesa', *Bulletin of the School of Oriental and African Studies*, vol. 51, no. 2 (1988).

Willis, Michael D., 'Architecture in Central India under the Kacchapaghata Rulers', South Asian studies 12 (1996).

Willis, Michael D., 'Some Notes on the Palaces of the Imperial Gurjara Pratiharas', *Journal of the Royal Asiatic Society*, vol. 5, no. 3 (1995).

Willis, Michael D., *Inscriptions of Gopaksetra: Materials for the History of Central India*, British Museum Press, 1996.

Willis, Michael D., *Temples of Gopaksetra: A Regional History of Architecture and Sculpture in Central India* AD *600–900*, British Museum Press, 1997.

Yadav, Rajendra, *Sculptural Art of Abaneri: A Paradigm*, Jawahar Kala Kendra, Jaipur, 2006.

INDEX